AF522412

STUDENT/SCHOOL ACHIEVEMENT

(Causes and Cure)

STUDENT/SCHOOL ACHIEVEMENT

(Causes and Cure)

By

Dr. B.C. Mishra

M.Phil., Ph.D., DDE, PGDHE(IGNOU)

Senior Lecturer in Education

D.P.I.A.S.E., Berhampur

Dist. Ganjam (Orissa)

and

Dr. Pradeep Kumar Danga

M.Phil., Ph.D.,

Lecturer in Education

DAV CTE, Koraput, (Orissa)

DISCOVERY PUBLISHING HOUSE

NEW DELHI

First Published–2005

ISBN 81-7141-987-9

Published by:

DISCOVERY PUBLISHING HOUSE

4831/24, Prahlad Street, Ansari Road, Darya Ganj
New Delhi–110 002 (India)
Phone: 23279245, • Fax: 91-11-23253475
e-mail: dphtemp@indiatimes.com

Printed at:
Amit Enterprises, Delhi

Preface

Academic achievement is of paramount importance, particularly in the present socio-economic and cultural contexts. Achievement is the end-product of all educational endeavours. The main concern of all educational efforts is to see that the learner achieves. Quality control, quality assurance and, of late, total quality management of achievement have increasingly gained the attention of researchers in education. After exploring the concept of achievement in the cognitive, affective and psychomotor aspects of human behaviour, researchers have probed further and have attempted to understand the 'black box' of achievement. The studies on 'how' of achievement have brought to light the correlates of achievement and paved the way for control and manipulation of variables for quality management of achievement.

The distressing phenomena scholastic underachievement and failure have been causing serious concern to educationists, guidance counselors and educational planners for several decades as these amount to colossal wastage of resources available for education in our country. This necessities serious probe into the causes that underlie and factors that lead to underachievement and failure so that means could be devised to grapple with this enormous problem.

The present volume is the report of a study conducted systematically in the area of student achievement and allied aspects. The whole work has been arranged in eight chapters. The first chapter focuses on conceptualisation of self-concept and adjustment. The relevance of the study has been highlighted in the second chapter. Studies on various aspects pertinent to the study occupy their place in the third chapter. The fourth chapter delineates the design adopted for the conduct of the study. It incorporates the reference of the methodology, tools used and organization of data generated through team. It is followed by three chapters devoted to empirical analysis of data and their interpretation. The former twos (i.e. chapters 5 and 6) present the picture of student's self-concept and adjustment in relation to sex, residential background, academic stream and the level of achievement respectively. The later (Chapter 7) gives an account of the interrelationship among the variables. The last chapter embodies the findings of the study from which emanate certain relevant conclusions. In the end a few suggestions for further exploring the field have also been enumerated.

The study makes some deep probe on the much needed phenomenon of student achievement and brings about educational implications to augment the present educational scenario. The authors would feel amply rewarded if it could encourage educational researchers and planners to take up the challenge of revamping school education.

The authors sincerely believe the educationists, teachers, educational planners and researchers will find this book relevant to their fields of activity.

We are thankful to all those authors and publishers whose works have been cited in this study.

The authors would like to appreciate the cooperation of the respondents while collecting data. At the end we extend our thanks to Mr. Tilak Raj Wasan, Discovery Publishing House, New Delhi, for undertaking the publication of this book.

Berhampur **Brundaban Chandra Mishra**
The 15th January, 2005 **Pradeep Kumar Danga**

Contents

Introduction

The tremendous and accelerating advances of modern science and technology have led to unprecedented progress and unprecedented problems. On the one had, we can point to man's increasing mastery of the secrets of nature, to an economy of abundance, to the conquest of disease, and to spectacular cultural advances; on the other, we see the dangers of a divided world, of thermonuclear warfare, of a population explosion, of grinding poverty side by side with abundance, and of other complex problems which man has never before faced. These problems press for solution if man is to survive and move forwards, and the solution to these problems appears to depend less upon increased technological know-how and more upon a better understanding of man and his social systems. The impact of the scientific age upon the hopes and fears of man has been well described by Cantril (1958):

> "As more and more people throughout the world become more and more enmeshed in a scientific age, its psychological consequences on their thought and behaviour become increasingly complicated. The impact comes in a variety of ways, people begin to feel the potentialities for a more abundant life that modern technology can provide; they become aware of the inadequacies of many present political, social and religious institutions and practices, they discern the threat which existing power and status relationships may hold to their own development; they vaguely sense the inadequacy of many of the beliefs and codes accepted by their forefathers and perhaps by themselves at an earlier age.

The upshot is that more and more people are acquiring both a hope for a better life and a feeling of frustration and anxiety that they themselves may not experience the potentially better life they feel should be available to them. They search for new anchorage's, for new guidelines, for plans of action which hold a promise of making some of the dreams come true, some of their aspirations become experimentially real."

Life is a series of adjustments. Every moment the individuals are subjected to various situations of stress or strain or conflict, which makes it imperative to seek adjustment to the situation in order to release the tension. Just as biological adjustment is needed for physical survival of the organism, social adjustment is needed for individual growth, gratification and success in life. It is in this sense that adjustment becomes a process of Learning. Students who are continuously in conflict with parental demands and restrictions and who encounter inhibiting situation at home and hence consider it to be a prison and source of frustration rather than a place of security and affection, will find it difficult to maintain their academic life and standard. Students who fail to attain a satisfactory level of social adjustment will have difficulties in school. As a matter of fact, the development of healthy personality is largely determined by the way in which the individual is able to make adjustments in his life. It is in this sense that the very concept of personality is defined in terms of the individual's process of dynamic organisation of his psycho-physical systems for effective and unique adjustment to the environment (Allport 1962). A growing child has to successfully effect adjustment in various aspects of his life like home, health, personal, academic, emotional, social, school, vocation and so on. Hurlock (1955) recognized the period of adolescence as a period of adjustment and says that it is a period of maturing.

The extent and the mode of one's adjustment depend on one's own motivation for a successful life in terms of his aspirations. The period of adolescence is also considered to be a period of day dreaming where in the students would be entertaining various types of unrealistic aspirations, which perhaps adds to their adjustment problems.

The purpose of education is to enable a child to lead a better life in the future and to enjoy fully the potentialities it possesses. It is very sad that a section of our society, the children of scheduled caste people, come to school with a basic social disability due to which they encounter more problems that the normal children without any social disability. In order to improve the statue of these groups of people the government and other social agencies are doing a lot, by giving a number of concessions as also by giving education, by starting residential institutions for them and running special classes for their sake. Yet the students themselves have to built up within themselves a positive attitude and confidence only then they would be able to make proper adjustment with the environment and its challenges.

Personality of an individual consists of his persistent tendencies to make adjustment between his needs and environment. A balanced personality is the outcome of proper adjustment of an individual of his social environment. Psychologically adjustment may be defined as a process by means of which an individual makes an effort to establish equilibrium. Maladjustment leads to various personality complexities. It affects academic achievement and intelligence. Adjustment means how efficiently an individual can perform his duties in different circumstances, business, education, medical professional, military etc. and other social activities require efficient and well adjusted men for the progress of the nation. A person, who is comfortable with his inner life and inter-personal relations and has no difficulty in performing the roles and tasks expected of him, is relatively well adjusted.

SELF-CONCEPT: A CONCEPTUAL ANALYSIS

The study of 'self and self-concept' has attracted the attention of psychologists and educationists for quite sometime past now. It has been suggested that the overall performance of a pupil is largely dependent on his self-concept. In recent years, two types of influences have tended to lever out the traditional notion that human conduct can not be understood in all its richness and creativity without regarding it as issuing from a self, which is revealed in overt and observable behaviour patterns. One such influence has been the tendency to reject psychological concepts based on philosophical assumptions. However, compelling, and to construe psychological theory on empirically verifiable data. The notion of the self thus gave way to such concepts as 'personality traits', dimensions of personality and the like, which lent themselves to statistical formulation, objective measurement and assessment in quantitative terms.

Another influence which has exercised a far-reaching effect on modern psychological theory has emerged from phenomenal advance in the areas of electro, physiology and neurosurgery. It is claimed by those who believe that they have gained new insights into the nature of brain processes that all facts of human behaviour are capable of being explained and understood strictly in physiological terms. The little gap which co-exists on account of the incompleteness of our present knowledge of the brain will soon close as our knowledge of cerebral processes advances. In the face of this, there is no need in the opinion of some neuropsychiatrists, to talk of a 'self' or 'ego' which functions as an unifying or coordinating force, integrating that variety and diversity which characterizes what is objectively known regarding human behaviour.

On both counts, the notion of 'self' has been relegated to the province of philosophical speculation, with no justification in terms of the empirical concepts of modern science. Many contemporary psychologists prefer to interpret human behaviour in terms of 'hierarchies of habits', 'operant conditioning process', 'object cathaxes' 'personality predisposition's' and the like, with no need for any reference to the self as a background against which the changing scence, of human life must be viewed.

Despite the position of secondary importance accorded in modern thinking to the concept of the self, there is a growing realiztion today that this concept is not wholly irrelevant to the quest of the contemporary psychologists. The unending history of man's curiosity about the causes of his conduct, and the question of a psychic force which initiates, regulates, guides and shapes human action and behaviour has been ceaselessly raised, debated and discussed. It is in a sense inescapable that the concept of an inner entity soul, immortal, free and of divine origin-should have engaged the attention of so many thinkers of East and West, and that they should have accepted the critical role of the self as a principal controlling agent which shapes human destiny. In truth, self is the nucleus of human personality.

CHANGING FOCUS ON SELF

The concept of 'self' has long past but a short history. This field in educational research has not yet been extensively or intensively explored by the researchers or even self-psychsiologists for that matter. The formation of "self-concept" is a continuous and life-long process and it is related basically to the problem of thinking. The way one thinks about oneself and constructs an image of oneself that gets projected are important in this regard.

The role perception of an individual through image building very much influences the concept of 'self'. Human behaviour is a very complex process and as such is very difficult to understand and predict. But self-concept has become an important means in the recent years to understand, interpret and predict it.

Rogers (1951) believed that 'self' is a basic factor in the formation of personality and in determining hehaviour but according to him it had interred the field of psychology as a problem of research in the later quarter of 19th century, As early as 1890 William James, developed the notion of 'self' around which he could construct a grand picture of mental life. Such a notion of self gave way to concepts such as 'personality traits', and the dimension of personality, which eventually led towards statistical formulations, objective measurement and assessment in quantitative terms.

In the modern age, 'self-concept' has been recognized as a potent means for making a deep study of personality as it helps in understanding human behaviour. It is now believed that self is a principal controlling agent, which shapes human destiny. In reality 'self' is viewed by the majority of self-psychologists as the nucleus of human body.

Thus, the self is not only related to motivational activity alone, but act as a regulating and coordinating factor in perceiving, learning, remembering, planning, risk taking, judging and in decision taking matters or situations. While solving a problem or in undertaking some work, the level of performance is determined not only by the difficulty or case of the problem, but also by the image one has built about oneself in general. When one grows, one learns about one's reciprocities with others as high, low, friendly or unfriendly, dominant or subordinate.

SELF–A PSYCHOLOGICAL EXPLANATION

William James (1980) was the first to analyse 'self' in terms of its constituents Later Baldwin (1895) gave an interactionist account and attempted the study of 'self' on a scientific footing. Cooley (1902) viewed 'self' through social interaction as a 'looking glass for the self'. Mead (1913) also adopted a similar approach based upon the lines indicated by Cooley and analysed the 'role-taking process of the self', Piaget and Wallen (1932) declared 'self' as the product of social interaction with the members of social or linguistic groups.

Koffka (1935) regarded 'self' as a nucleus of the ego and an executive, instead of an object or process. Chapman and Vokanan (1939) declared that the concept of self is a powerful determinant of one's level of aspiration. Lundholm (1940) made a clear-cut distinction between 'subjective self' and 'objective self'. According to him 'subjective self' presents symbols, words and self-awareness' and objective self consists of those symbol in terms of which other persons describe the individual.

It is curious to observe that he did not mention about 'ego' in this context. It was Chein (1944) who undertook a still finer distinction between 'self' and 'ego' by declaring that 'self' is what one is aware of, while 'ego' is a group of processes.

Late Murphy (1947) propounded the idea of 'self' as the individual known to the individual.

Around the same time Hilgard (1949) emphasized the study of the 'inferred self' while the phenomenologists like Combs and Snygg (1949) maintained the phenomenal self includes all those parts of the phenomenal field, which the individual experience as characteristics himself. It may be noted that views of such self-psychologists appear to have shifted in favour of the importance of 'self' both as an object and process and efforts were made to provide the concept of 'self' as a suitable and meaningful place in the scheme of things.

SELF AS OBJECT AND PROCESS

Researchers concerned with the study of personality have tried to conceptualize behaviour in terms of single unified process, where many theorists have utilized the notion of self-concept. Lindzey and Hall (1957) suggested that the term 'self' has come to connote two distinct meanings to psychologists, self-as-object and self-as-process. Self-as-object may be defined simply as the aggregate of attitude, feelings, judgements and values which an individual holds with respect to this behaviour, his ability, his worth as a person, in short, how he perceives and evaluate himself. Self-as-process is defined in terms of activities such as thinking, perceiving and coping with the environment.

Some individuals have used the term 'ego' to denote the same construct. The self-concept described in terms of self-as-object is considered to be a potent aspect of personality and that individual differences are regarded as meaningful as differences in abilities, values, motives and attitudes. The self-as-process governs behaviour and adjustment.

SHADES OF PSYCHOLOGICAL OPINION: 'SELF' AND 'EGO'

In developing the concept of self as distinct from ego. William James (1980) analysed self in terms of its constituent parts—self feeling, and actions of self-seeking and self-preservation. The constituent parts of the self-included the sum total of what an individual considers to be his body, traits, characteristics, abilities, aspirations, family, work and other such affiliations. He further advanced the concept of the pure ego, which was explained in terms of the stream of consciousness constituting one's sense of personal identity. Regarding the concept of self-based on the theory pronounced by James (1980). Some prefer to treat the respective concept of self and ego as separate. There are some who have no objection to the use of these two terms interchangeably. Thus, according to Koffka (1935) self is the core of nucleus of the ego and the ego is conceptualized both as doer and object.

Chein (1944) made reference to the prevalent view of self and ego. According to him self is what one is aware of, where, as ego is a group of processes. The motives and ideas of the ego serve the purpose of defending, extending, enhancing and preserving the self. The threat to the self is sought to be countered by the ego. He feels that self is though to be a part of the total personality of an individual. The self follows a course of continuous development and growth and becomes more and more complex and involved with the emerging of individual into adulthood.

According to Bertocci (1945) 'self-process' is labelled 'self' and 'self-as-object' is called 'ego' following the traditional meanings attached to these two terms. His use of the term 'self' corresponds to Freud's (1935) use of the term ego as unitary activity of sensing, imagining, remembering, willing, feeling and thinking. The ego, as Bertocci conceived it, is a cluster of values which may become embodied in the form of traits with which the self identified its success rather similar to the use of this term by Sherif and Cantrill (1947) who are of the view that the ego is a constellation of attitudes for example, 'when I think of myself, what I value, what is mine and what I identify with'.

Thus, their ego is something more than self-as-object, for if the ego becomes involved, it motivates behaviour. As set forth by them ego involved behaviour is more effective than its noon-ego involved part. Inspite of their best efforts, the self-as-object and ego as process remain less differentiated and clear. Murphy (1947) described 'self' as the individual known to the individual and 'ego' as group of activities concerned with the enhancement and defense of 'self'. Thus, self would consist of varied attitudes and feelings in regard to the person himself and ego would refer to associated processes and activities. In this framework, self is object, whereas ego is process.

In this way, those who distinguish between 'self' and 'ego' seem to be generally agreed on regarding self as entity and ego as a group of processes. Snygg and Combs (1949) talk of the phenomenal self, since all behaviour without exception is completely determined by and contingent on the phenomenal field of the behaving organism. Further they maintain that the phenomenal field consists of totality of experiences of which the individual is aware at the time of action. Varying awareness influences the behavour of the individual.

On this view the phenomenal self serves both as the object and the doer. It is doer because it is an aspect of phenomenal field, which determines all behaviour. It is also an object because it consists of self-experiences. Hilgard (1949) regards behaviour not as a product of the self but rather as a complex of psychological processes aroused by proximal and distal stimuli of which a person is largely unaware. He accords weightage to forces or factors outside the self.

Ausubel (1952) proposed a scheme of self made up primarily of perceptional ingredients whereas ego, according to him, consists of effectively charged conceptual ingredients such as self-ideals and self-values. Sarabin (1953) regarded self as a cognitive structure consisting of various aspects of an individuals being somatic, receptor, effector and social, since all these are based on experience, Sarabin speaks of the 'empirical-selves', using the term 'self' and 'ego' synonymously.

Shoben (1962) defined 'self' as a relatively stable organisation of values that mediates and focuses on that component of behaviour which influences very much every day life of human beings. Since he makes hardly any mention of ego. It may be presumed that he construes self both as object and doer.

Miller (1962) defined ego as the individual's conception of himself. He differentiated between ego and self still further. He laid stress on individual's conception of himself rather than on socially perceived self as reflected in other frames of references referred to earlier. It is obvious, therefore, that ego and self have been by and large considered to be two different concepts and there is now almost a consensus of opinion as to considering the ego in the sense of an executive and self as a group of attributes reflected in constellations of perceptions and attitudes of person about himself.

ROGERS THEORY OF 'SELF'

Rogers (1951) who was influenced by the theory of phenomenal self believed that in addition to the self-structure there is an ideal self which indicates what the person would like to do. For him the self or self-concept denotes the organized, consistent and a conceptual gestalt composed of perceptions of the characteristics of 'I' on 'ME' and the perceptions of relationship of 'I' and 'ME' to others and the various aspects of life together with the values attached to these perceptions. It is regarded as a gestalt which is available to awareness though not necessarily in awareness thus, it is conceived of as a specific entity.

The theory of conceptual gestalt propounded by Rogers (1951) is perhaps the most important theory reported in the West. It differs from other Western theories of 'self' particularly of Freud and his dissenting associates emphasizing the 'self' as an 'I-ME' reaction of mental processes and other theories of self referring to 'I-ME' reactions of individual because Rogers concept of 'self' apart from individuals 'I-ME' also. Rogers argues that the 'self' is a basic factor in the formation of personality and in the determination of behaviour. The phenomenological theory of self an advanced by Rogers relies heavily upon the concept of 'self' as an explanatory concept.

It may be observed that the study of 'self-concept' could get the necessary the fillip for making depth study of personality partly due to the direct consequence and bearing of mental hygiene and clinical movement but more because of the realization that psychology without self cannot succeed in knowing human behaviour.

Rogers (1951) theory of 'self' influenced clinical psychology and special perception. Hall and Lindzey (1957) explained the chief conceptual ingredient of Rogers theory of 'self' as under

- The organism is a total individual
- The phenomenal field is the totality of experience, and
- The self is differentiated portion of the phenomenal field and consists of a pattern of conscious perceptions and values of 'I' or 'ME.'

It may be worthwhile to point out that the nuclear concept of Rogers theory of personality is the self which has numerous properties and some may be indicated as under

- It develops out of the organisms interaction with the environment.
- It may interject the value of other people and perceive them in a distorted fashion.
- The self strives for consistency.
- The organism behaves in ways that are consistent with the self.
- Experiences which are not consistent with the self structure are perceived as threats.
- The self may change as a result of maturation and learning.

Rogers (1951) discussed the nature of these concepts and their inter-relationships in a series of nineteen propositions formulated by him. Accordingly he made the self an object of empirical research and changed the theoretical status of self given by the psychologists previously. It is interesting to note that he proposed a theory of personality development, a personality functioning and personality change with the concept of self as its central focus.

SELF–A CENTRE

"The Self" is considered as that segment of an individual, which is known to an individual. It is one's own image in one's own eyes, as perceived, felt and thought of by onself. One perceives others and can perceive oneself also, but this perception of one and others cannot be objective and correct. For an individual his own self is at the core of everything that matters. A person behaves in accordance with the self. Two things are assumed to be vital in the life of an individual—the concept of 'self' and perception of the environment. The other reality, however objective it may be, shall not effect the behaviour of a person unless it gets to self.

EVOLUTION OF 'SELF'

In tracing the evolution of the self-concept it may be observed at the outset that psychologists drawn towards it believe that the self of a person develops from birth onwards through the process of differences between 'ME' and 'not ME'. It was regarded as the outcome of the product of interaction from infancy with an individual's physical and social environment.

Baldwin (1895) thought that the ego and the alter are thus born together. Cooley (1902) and Mead (1903) developed the concept of self as based on social interaction. Piaget (1932) conceived of the self as a product of interaction with others. Sarabin (1953) as pointed out earlier believed in three aspects of one's self-somatic, receptor-effector and social. According to him the child continues to incorporate new classification and qualities during his life span. It has been observed and proved from many cases of prolonged isolation in childhood that the formation of self depends upon interaction with other persons. It is in this course of interaction that the child develops the self-attitude in his life.

Sherif and Sherif (1956) observed that consistency in competing with others in comparing with others, in experiencing sympathy with another's distress, in responsibility for self. Also setting of goals on one's own performance appears gradually as the child participates in social and co-operative forms of play as contrasted with side by side or parallel play. In this way the child achieve adulthood and becomes a socialized member of the society. Due to body's growth and change in life, a transition in the self-concept also occurs from childhood to old age.

Dinkmeyer (1965) has laid emphasis on the development character of the self and describe that the interaction continues throughout the life and is linked with the mood, familiar sensations, pleasure, pain, resistance, acceptance, rejection and gratification with the passage of time. As the child grows, he learns about the world and also about himself. Thus, three inferences may be adduced evidently in respect of self development from the above explanation. First, the self is a developmental formation in the psychological process of the individual Secondly, the self consists of interrelated and acquired aspects of life. Thirdly, the individual's relations to others are defined to be regulated by self in various concrete situations and activities.

PARAMETERS OF 'SELF'

The self analyses have been attempted with four major dimensions popularly known as perceived self, real self, social self and ideal self. They are briefly being explained as follows.

Perceived Self

Perceived self simply implies what a person thinks he is. This is influenced by the physical self of the person, his physical appearances, his dress and grooming, his abilities and dispositions, his values and his beliefs and aspirations. Thus, it represents traits of ones' nature which have been detected and integrated into a pattern. It constitutes the idea or concept one forms about oneself. Perceived self is often called self-concept of an individual Southerland (1956) referred to it as the individual known to the individual. It is his 'I' and 'ME' his constant frame of reference, the proud possession which he wants to maintain and enhance at all costs. This part of individual's makeup determines his behavioural expressions. Sullivan (1953) suggested that the self-concept as a unit has many facets of a dynamic equilibrium.

Real-Self

Real-self means what the person really is. It is also includes what the individual is aware of and as such it is characteristics of the person as assessed objectively or as seen sometimes by other people. This self is also called the perceived self plus unconscious self.

Social-Self

This refers to the self as one thinks or others view it. The concept may not correspond with others perceptions of himself. But even then this self has very major effect upon one's behaviour. It is actually the self as looked upon or estimated by persons other than the individual himself.

Ideal-Self

This self tends to mean what an individual thinks he would like to be. Butler and Haigh (1954) observed that the ideal self implies the organized conceptual patterns of characteristics and emotional states which an individual consciously holds desirable or undesirable for himself. It is also presumed that an individual is able to order his self-perception. 'What I like to be' and 'What I would least like to be'. This type of dimensional division of the 'self' is done only for the sake of convenience and exploration into its nature. But for all practical purposes 'self' is one singly entity. Some investigators have resorted to the use of 'ideal-self' as means of determining the self aspirations of the persons. This concept has been shown to be valuable in determining the relationship between how the person sees himself and what he thinks he should be like.

It may be noted that Havighurst, Robinson and Dorr (1946) hypothesized the ideal self to be development in nature and suggested that the ideal self begins when the child identified with a parental figure. They also indicated that during middle childhood and early adolescence it moves through a stage of romanticism and glamour, and culminates in late adolescence as a composite of desirable characteristics which may be symbolized by an attractive, real and visible young adult as perhaps even an imaginary person. This classification of the self has helped in revealing many interesting facets.

The discrepancies between the different aspect of 'self' are essential for purposes of understanding and evaluating an individual completely. Thus, the difference in real self and perceived self is known as 'self-insight'. It is just possible that an individuals' perceive self may not correspond to his ideal-self and if the difference between these two selves is found to be less, the individual will undoubtedly be better adjusted and vice versa. Many researches have been done to bring to light this fact. Talyor and Combs (1952), Bills and Vance (1953), Zimmer (1954) and Zukerman and Monashkur (1957) have done interesting studies in this field. Sharma and others (1967) observe that self acceptance can also be as effectively measured positive negative dimension as perceived ideal self discrepancies.

COMPONENTS OF SELF-CONCEPT

According to Hurlock (1974) the concept of self has three major components, the perceptual, the conceptual and the attitudinal. The perceptual component is similar to physical self-concept, which includes the image of one's appearance, attractiveness and sex appropriateness of body and the importance of different parts of body. The conceptual component is similar to psychological self-concept, which relates to the origin of the individual, his abilities and disabilities, his social adjustment and traits of personality.

The attitudinal component refers to attitudes of a person about his present status and future prospects, his feelings about his worthiness, his attitudes of self-esteem and pride and shame. It also includes his beliefs, convictions and values.

SELF-CONCEPT-BEHAVIOURAL DETERMINANT

An individual behaviour is a function of his 'self-concept' and depends upon the way in which he perceives the situation. Adler (1931), Snygg and Combs (1949), Klockhohn and Murray (1953), Rogers and Dymond (1954) and Mccandless (1962) have established the fact that an individual behaves in a particular situation according to his 'self-concept' and that 'self-concept' of an individual dictates and directs his response in any setting. Adler, as early as 1931 observed how the feelings of inferiority (components of self concept) affect and individual behavior and his attitudes towards the society and situation in the family. Snygg and Combs (1949) suggests that behaviour is entirely dependent on organism's perceptual field which means the entire universe, as it is experienced by the individual at the time of action.

Thus, behaviour and 'self-concept' interact with each other and influence each other. Bugental and Cunning (1955) state that the success with the individual adjusts to the problems of adults life if bound to have some influence upon his 'self-concept'. They have found a positive correlation between successfully adjustments and stable 'self-concept'. An individuals behaviour is dictated by his self-concept in a particular situation and is influenced directly and indirectly by this. Thus, it may be taken to imply that 'self-concept' plays a vital role in the behaviour determination of an individual.

SELF AS AN ACTUALISOR

Maslow (1968) has developed a new thesis by formulating a paradigm showing a hierarchical nature of need-mix to support it. According to him the two higher needs viz., self-esteem and self-actualization are dependent on the fulfillment of basis physiological needs, safety needs for love and belongingness. The emphasis has been laid on the highest type of need in this scale which refers to self-actualisation. Maslow (1943) assumed that those needs, which have the greatest potency at any given time dominate behaviour and demand satisfaction. The individual feels driven so to say by a high priority need. Klhen the need is satisfied, a high order motive (need) makes its appearance and demands its satisfaction, and soon to the top of the hierarchy. The highest need, which is called 'self-actualisation' is defined by Maslow as follows:

> "A Musician must make music, an artist must paint, a poet must write, if he is ultimately to be at place with himself, what a man can be, he must be. This need we may call self-actualization."

It may be observed that 'self-actualization' need not take the form of creative characteristics of a genius. A fine mother, an athlete, a good workman or a teacher may be actualizing their potentialities in doing well, what they can do best. It is never the less true that 'self-actualisers' are comparatively rare and this proportionately represented among the gifted. Most of us apparently are seeking satisfaction of lower order needs.

ADJUSTMENT—THE CONCEPT

People react to their personal conflicts and frustrations and to the demands of the environment in divergent ways. These reactions, according to Schineiders (1955) are known as 'patterns of adjustment' such an approach has to do with the kind of responses that a person makes to whatever problems, difficulties or demands he encounters. Another approach complementary to this is concerned with the study of human adjustment from the stand-point of the situational context of the response. This involves finding out how does the person responds to his home and family, to school to himself and to his social environment.

Adjustment is a process that helps a person to lead a happy and contended life while maintaining a balance between his needs and his capacity to fulfill them. It enables him to change his way of life according to the demands of the situation and gives him the strength and ability to bring about the necessary changes in the conditions of his environment.

In addition to his own basic needs, an individual is also subject to certain demands of society. If one thinks only in terms of satisfying his own needs without thought of the norms, ethics and cultural-traditions of society, he will not be adjusted to his environment. Adjustment does not cater only to one's own demands but also to the demands of the society. It may, therefore, be stated that in its comprehensive connotation, adjustment is a condition or state in which the individuals behavior conforms to the demands of the culture or society to which he belongs and he feels that his own needs have been, or will be fulfilled. Thus, in addition to the pattern of adjustment, there are varieties of adjustments like emotional, social and educational.

Crow and Crow (1956) pointed out that an individual's adjustment is adequate, wholesome or helpful to the extent that he has established harmonious relationship between himself and the conditions, situations and persons who comprise his physical and social environment.

The concept of adjustment implies a constant interaction between the persons and his environment, each making demands on the other. Sometimes adjustment is accomplished when the person yields and accepts conditions, which are beyond his power to change. Sometimes it is achieved when the environment yields to the person's constructive activities. In most cases adjustment is a compromise between these two extremes and maladjustment is a failure to achieve a satisfactory compromise (White, 1956).

According to Good (1959), adjustment is the process of finding and adopting modes of behaviour suitable to the environment or the changes in the environment.

Arkoff (1968) States

Adjustment is the interaction between a person and his environment. How one adjusts in a particular situation depends upon one's personal characteristics as also the circumstances of the situation. In other words, both personal and environmental factor work side by side in adjustment. An individual is adjusted if he is adjusted to himself and to his environment.

We can think of adjustment as psychological survival in much the same way as the biologist uses the term adaptation to describe physiological survival (Vonhaller, 1970).

Shaffer (1961) holds that adjustment is the process by which a living organism maintains a balance between its needs and the circumstances that influence the satisfaction of those needs.

ADJUSTMENT AS ACHIEVEMENT OR PROCESS

Adjustment can be interpreted as both, process and the outcome of that process in the form of some attainment or achievement. When a poor child studies under the street light because he has not lighting arrangement at home he is said to be in a process of adjustment. What he attains in terms of success in his examination of the fulfillment of his ambition or pride in his achievement is nothing but the result of his adjustment to his self and his environment. Thus, adjustment as an achievement means how the effectiveness with which an individual can function in changed circumstances and is, as such, related to his adequacy and regarded as an achievement that is accomplished either badly or well (Lazarus, 1976).

Adjustment as a process describes and explains the ways and means of an individual's adoption to his self and his environment without reference to the quality of such adjustment or its outcome in terms of success or failure. It only shows how individuals or a group or groups of people cope under changing circumstances and what factors influence this adjustment. Let us now consider some salient features of adjustment as an interaction between a person and his environment.

Continuous process—The process of adjustment is continuous. It starts at once birth and goes on without stop till one's death. A person as well as his environment are constantly changing as also are his needs in accordance with the demands of the changing external environment. Consequently, the process or terms of an individual's adjustment can be expected to change from situation to situation and according to Arkoff (1968), there is nothing like satisfactory or complete adjustment which can be achieve once and for all time. It is something that is constantly achieved and richened by us.

Two-Way Process

Adjustment is a two-way process and involves not only the process of fitting oneself into available circumstances but also the process of changing the circumstances to fit one's needs. The concept of adjustment implies a constant interaction between the person and his environment, each making demands on the other. Sometimes adjustment is accomplished when the person yields and accepts conditions, which are beyond his power to change. Sometimes it is achieved when the environment yields to the person's constructive activities. In most cases adjustment is a compromise between these two extremes and maladjustment is a failure to achieve a satisfactory compromise (White, 1956).

AREA OF ADJUSTMENT

Adjustment in the case of an individual should consist of personal as well as environmental components. These two aspects of adjustment can be further subdivided into smaller aspects of personal and environmental factors. Adjustment, although seeming to be a universal characteristic or quality may have different aspects and dimension.

Through the numerous efforts at measuring adjustment through inventories and other techniques, these aspects have been identified and various tests have been constructed to assess their dimensions. For example, Bell (1958) has taken five areas or dimensions in his adjustment inventory namely, home, health, social, emotional and occupational.

Arkoff (1968) in his book: Adjustment and Mental Health has enumerated the family, school or college, vocation and marriage as the important areas of adjustment.

Recently, Joshi and Pandey (1964), in their research study covering school and college students, have given 11 areas or dimensions of an individual's adjustment:

1. Health and physical development.
2. Finance, living conditions and employment.
3. Social and recreational activities.
4. Courtship, sex and marriage.
5. Social psychological relations.
6. Personal psychological relations.
7. Moral and religious.
8. Home and family.
9. Future-vocational and education.
10. Adjustment to school and college work.
11. Curriculum and teaching.

In this way, adjustment of a person is based on the harmony between his personal characteristics and the demands of the environment of which he is a part. Personal and environmental factors work side by side in brining about this harmony.

MODELS OF ADJUSTMENT

Some people adjust to their environment while others do no, what are the factors that make an individual adjusted or maladjusted? There are several theories and models describing the pattern of adjustment for answering such questions. Let us discuss some of the important models.

1. Moral Model

This represents the oldest view-point about adjustment or maladjustment. According to this view, adjustment or maladjustment should be judged in terms of morality, i.e., absolute norms of expected behaviour. Those who follow the norms are adjusted (Virtuous or good people) and those who violate or do not flow these norms are maladjusted (Sinners). Evil supernatural forces like demons, devils etc. were blamed for making one indulge in behaviour against the norms (committing sins). While the religious gods, goddess and other saintly great souls were responsible for making one a happy, healthy, prosperous and pious person (adjusted in the modern sense). However, as the medical and biological sciences advanced and scientific reasoning gained a firm footing in the nineteenth century, the moral model was replaced by the medico-biological model.

2. The Medico-Biological Model

This model holds, genetic, physiological and biochemical factors responsible for a person being adjusted or maladjusted to his self and his environment. Maladjustment, according to the model, is the result of disease in the tissue of the body, especially the brain. Such disease can be the result of heredity or damage acquired during the course of a person's life—by injury, infection, or hormonal disruption arising from stress, among other things. In the opinion of Lazaras (1976), the correction of adjustive failure or disorders requires correction of the tissue defect through physical therapies such as drugs, surgery and the like.

This model is still extent and enjoys credibility for rooting out the causes of adjustive failure in terms of genetic influence, bio-chemical defect hypotheses and disease in the tissues of the body. However, it is not correct to assign physiological or organic causes to all maladapted and malfunctioning behaviour, especially when there is no evidence of physiological malfunction. Such a situation certainly calls for other explanations, view points or models.

3. The Psychoanalytic Model

This model owes its origin to the theory of psychoanalysis propagated by Sigmoid Freud (1938) and supported by psychologists like Adler, Jung and other neo-Freudians.

A. *Freud's Views*

According to Freud following are the factors which are relevant to success or failure in adjustment.

1. The human psyche or mind consists of three layers, the conscious, the sub-conscious and unconscious. The unconscious holds the key to our behaviour. It decides the individuals adjustment and maladjustment to his self and to his environment. It contains all the repressed wishes, desires, feelings, drives and motives many of which are related to sex and aggression. One is adjusted or maladjusted to the degree, extent or the ways in which these are kept dominant or under control.
2. According to Freud, man is a pleasure seeking animal by nature. He wants to seek pleasure and avoid pain or anything which is not in keeping with his pleasure loving nature. The social restrictions imposed by the mores of society an his own moral standards dictated by his superego come in conflict with the unrestricted and unbridled desired of his basis pleasure seeking nature. These pleasures are mostly sexual in nature. One remains adjusted to the extent that these are satisfied. An individual drifts towards malfunctioning of behaviour and maladjustment in case such satisfaction is threatened or denied. Freud postulated the imaginary concepts of 'id', 'ego' and 'super ego' for the adjustive and non-adjustive behaviour patterns and formulated the following conclusion.

A person's behaviour remains normal and in harmony with this self and his environment to the extent that his ego is able to maintain the balance between the evil designs of his id and the moral ethical standard dictated by his super ego. In case the ego is strong enough to exercise proper control over one's id and super ego, malfunction of behaviour would result. Two different situation could then arise:

(a) If the super ego dominates then there is no acceptable outlet for expression of the repressed wishes, impulses and appetities of the id. Such a situation maybe given birth to neurotic tendencies in the individual.

(b) If the id dominates, then the individual pursues his unbridled pleasure seeking impulses, without care for the social and moral norms. In such a situation the individual may be seen to be engaged in unlawful or immoral activities resulting in maladaptive, problem or delinquent behaviour.

3. Freud also uses the concept of libido, i.e., a flow of energy related to sex gratification. He equates it with a flowing river and maintain that:

(a) If its flow is outward causing sex gratification and pleasurable sensation from outside objects, the individual remains quite normal and adjusted to his self and the environment.

(b) Its inward flow leads to self-indulgence and narcissism.

(c) If its path is blocked, this results in its arrest leading to regressive behaviour, a kind of abnormality.

(d) If the flow of the libido is dammed up, condemned or repressed through the authority exercises by the ego in association with the superego, it may cause severe maladjustment. When the ego is weak and the super ego is rigid, this may lead to psychotic personality disorders. However, when the ego is weak and the superego also is not too rigid it may result in relatively simple disorders like neurosis or still simpler maladaptive behaviour characterized by restlessness, sleeplessness, headache, stomachache, backache, vomiting, lack of appetite etc.

4. According to Freud, adjustment or maladjustment should not be viewed only in terms of what the individual may be undergoing at present and what happened to him in his earlier childhood is even more important. What he may have experienced a as a child, what types of gratification to his sex urge he has achieved, what has been repressed in his unconscious, how he has passed through the distinct stages of sexual development etc. are, thus, quite important for making him adjusted or maladjusted to his self and the environment.

B. *Adler's Views*

Adler disagreed with his teacher, and substituted the sex motive with the power motive or desire to attain superiority and perfection to explain human behaviour. He maintained that:

(i) There is an inherent strong urge in all human beings to seek power and attain superiority. Besides this as a child, one is helpless and dependent which makes one feel inferior and inorder to make up for the feelings of inferiority, one takes recourses to compensatory behaviour, i.e. indulges in a struggle for power. Environmental situations, constitutional deficiency and many other factors may also make one feel inferior and to get away from these feelings one learns to struggle for achieving power. An individuals efforts for seeking power of attaining perfection may also be the result or his need for creative expression, the urge to do something new, to enhance his status in the eyes of his colleagues and others.

(ii) Stimulated thus by the urge to seek power or attain superiority and perfection, one adopt a distinctive lifestyle suited to one's environmental situations. One continues to strive for superiority by emulating and exploiting the ways and means provided by one's lifestyles. Adjustment or the lack of it would

depend on whether one's effort end in success or failure to achieve one's goal. Thus, the following three situations may arise.

(a) Success in seeking gratification of one's power motive or attaining superiority may lead to good adjustment to one's self and the environment.

(b) In the case of partial failure, if one is successful in bringing about a slight modification in one's life goals or style of life one may be able to reconcile with ones' self and the environment and may feel adjusted and remain normal.

(c) In case of failure to obtain gratification of the power motive and to change one's goal or style of life, one may drift towards non-adjustive or maladjustive behaviour leading to mild on severe mental illness.

C. *Jung's Views*

Jung's system of analytical psychology advocated the idea of the self-actualization motive instead of Freud's sex gratification motive and Adler's power seeking motive for explaining the why and how of human behaviour. According to him, one has a strong inner urge or motive of exhibit one's talents or abilities or seek self-actualization. Accordingly one utilizes one's life energy, i.e., the flow of libido as a channel for self-expression to satisfy the urge for self-actualization. The degree of adjustment of one's personality depends on the extent to which one is successful in actualizing oneself. Libido, the life energy as Jung maintains may flow both ways—inward or outward, turning in individual into an introvert or extrovert personality. In the introvert, thinking is predominant while sensations and feelings are suppressed. In the extroverts, on the other hand, the feelings or sensations are more predominant and the thinking is suppressed. Generally speaking however, an individual is neither purely introvert not a purely extrovert. He is ambivert, i.e. while showing the symptoms of an introvert, he possesses some characteristics of the extrovert and vice versa. As long as a person can maintain a proper balance between his thinking and feeling he remains adjusted to his self and the environment. But lopsided behaviour, i.e. laying too much emphasis on thinking at the cost of feelings or giving too much consideration to feelings at the cost of thinking may disturb the balance of one's psyche. It may lead to maladaptive behaviour causing mld or severe mental illness.

Another criterion for normal or properly adoptive behaviour according to Jung's theory, is the reconciliation between one's conscious and unconscious behaviour. Failure on one's part to maintain or achieve such reconciliation may lead to maladaptive behaviour and mental illness. When one's conscious is not in tune with the unconscious or when the unconscious turns hostile on account of being not properly understood by the conscious it is bound to create imbalances in one's mind and make one's behaviour quite hostile to one self and to one's environment. If this hostility or aggression is directed in ward, one becomes neurotic but when it overflows outwards, one turns into a psychotic or delinquent character. In some severe forms of insanity, as claimed by Jung, we find a complete autonomy of the unconscious a type of complete control or bombardment of the conscious mind by the unconscious contents in the shape of disturbing and unusual ideas. Harmony or discord between one's conscious and unconscious may thus proves to be a deciding factor for one's personality to be termed as adjustment or maladjusted to one's self and the environment.

The views of other neo-Freudians and later psycho-analysists—the other followers of the psychoanalysis school also tried to put forward their own view points explaining the why and how of human behaviour. Noteable among them were Karen Horney, Erich Fromm, Wilhelm Reich and Erick H. Erickson. Their views are briefly discuss below.

D. *Karen Horney's Views*

While Adler thought the need for power (to counter the feelings of inferiority) to be the root cause of human behaviour, Horney (1937) placed emphasis on the need for security (to offset the feelings of anxiety). She postulated that an individual as a child feels helpless and isolated in a potentially hostile world. This creates some basic feelings of anxiety and the craving for security in him. A reasonable concern with security is normal. But if an individual is obsessed with security to the exclusion of self-development, he is likely to drift towards maladaptive or abnormal behaviour.

The anxious child, she further theorises, may ultimately move towards people and become dependent upon them, more against people and become hostile and rebellious, or move away from people and withdraw into himself. If a perso can integrate these three attitudes or responses, sometimes giving, sometimes fighting and sometimes keeping to himself, he may remain adjusted to his self and his environment. But in case he turns too much to one of these directions, regardless of the appropriateness in specific circumstances, he is bound to become maladjusted ending up with mild or severe mental illness or delinquent behaviour.

The other reason for maladjustment, according to Horney's theory, may be the denial or obstruction in the way of realizing one's need for self-esteem or self-realization. Anxiety is the result of situations where one starts by not valuing oneself highly enough. A conflict then arises between one's ideal self and the real self. An individual can remain adjusted and normal to the extent that the balance between these two selves is satisfactorily maintained and may drift towards abnormal or maladaptive behaviour if this is disturbed.

E. Erich Fromm's Views

Like Horney, Fromm also emphasizes the need of security and feels that as a child one may feel the necessity for belonging to offset the fear of isolated and aloneness. Consequently, the individual in his childhood may desire to live in the family, belonging to the members of the family and provided with love, affection and security by them. In due course, however, when he attains maturity he is impelled by an inner craving for freedom and as a result he tried to escape from the very bonds, which provided him the security he needed. In this kind of situation he may be confronted with the inner conflict of being dependent for the satisfaction of his need for security and his urge for freedom. This conflict is further heightened when parents and other members are also caught in the situation in the form of allowing independence to their progeny to play their roles as mature persons or trying to hold them back as a guarantee of their own future security. The extent to which this crisis of dependence versus independence or security versus freedom is resolved by the children with the help of their parents and elders, governs the degree to which their behaviour and functioning remain adjusted and normal. In case this crisis is not resolved satisfactorily, maladjustment and maladoption followed by mental illness and delinquent character formation may result.

F. *Wilhelm Reich's Views*

In agreement with Freud's views on the importance of sexuality, Reich firmly believed that an individual health both physical and psychological depends on the liberation of the sex drive, all the way to organism. However, from the day of birth, the release of libido or sexual energy is blocked by parents, teachers and society in general. Reich considers the term 'sexual energy' in a wider connotation calling it "Orgone energy" a life force energizing the total behaviour of an individual and responsible for all types of self expression. If this energy is properly channelized and flows along normal and natural ways, the individual remains adjusted and enjoys good physical and mental health, but in case the flow of this energy is blocked it may lead first to somatic or physical discomfort and then to the physiological and psychological disorder leading to mild or severe maladjustment and mental illness.

G. *Erickson's Views*

This contemporary psychoanalyst born in 1902, views adjustment as a function of the conflict between in born instincts and societal demands. He has divided the entire human life span into eight distinct stages. At each stage, the society characterized by a particular culture puts up a specific demand which may or may not suit the urges or instincts manifested at that specific stage by the individual.

In this way, at each stage of life one is faced with a crisis the resolution of which can have either a good or bad effect on one's adjustment. For example, during the stage of infancy, the individual is confronted with the problem of resolving the crisis peculiar to these stage, i.e., trust (enabling him to form intimate relationship) versus mistrust (enabling him to protect himself in the hostile world) for his proper growth and development. The outcome of his behaviour depends upon the success or failure of the satisfactory resolution of this crisis and consequently he may grow into a wholesome healthy personality or a defective and deviant personality.

4. The Sociogenic or Cultural Model

According to this model, the society in general and culture in particular affect's ones way of behaving to such an extent that behaviour takes the shape of adaptive or non-adaptive behaviour turning one into an adjusted or maladjusted personality. The society and culture to which one belongs does not only influence or shape one's behaviour but also set a standard for its adherents to behave in the way it desires. Individuals behaving in the manner that society desires are labeled as normal and adjusted individuals while deviation from social norms and violation of role expectancy is regarded as the sign of maladjustment and abnormality. Although society or culture plays a significant role in shaping and influencing human behaviour, yet it should not be regarded as the only factor in the adjustment process. Moreover, the societies or cultures may themselves, rather than the individual be maladaptive and sometimes even destructive to the individuals adjustment like Nazi Germany. It is not proper therefore, to depend solely on the sociogenic or cultural model for the labeling of one's behaviour as adjusted or maladaptive.

5. The Socio Psychological or Behaviouristic Model

The socio-psychological or behaviouristic model in general emphasizes that:

1. Behaviour is not inherited competencies required for successful living and largely acquired or learned through social experience by the individual himself.
2. The environmental influences provided by the culture and social institutions are important but it is the interaction of one's psychological self with one's physical as well as social environment which plays the decisive role in determining adjustive success or failure.
3. Behaviour, whether normal or abnormal is learned by obeying the same set of learning principles or laws. Generally every type of behaviour is learned or acquired as an after affect of its consequences. The behaviour ones occurred, if reinforced, may be learned by the individual as normal. As a result, one may learn to consider responses, which are labeled normal, as abnormal.
4. Not only is normal and abnormal behaviour learned, the labeling of behaviour as normal or abnormal is also learned. Whether or not an individual is considered abnormal or maladjusted for a particular type of behaviour depends upon the observer of the behaviour and also upon the social context of the behaviour.
5. Maladaptive behaviour may be treated by applying the principle of behaviour modification, unlearning, reconditioning and correcting environmental situations responsible for its occurrence.

All the models described above are true to certain extent (except the primitive model) for providing explanation for one's adjustive success or failure. But none of them is complete or adequate in itself for providing satisfactory explanation. Although medical or biological model, provides a sufficient basis for understanding mental illness or maladaptive behaviour resulting through organic causes, physical damage to the brain and genetic factors, yet it cannot be applied to the disorders due to psychological causes and societal factors. Adjustment must always be considered as a continuing product of one's interaction with the biological and social determinants lying in one's biological and genetic make-up and environmental set-up. It is, therefore, innate as well as learned. For its analysis the analyst has to prove into not only how an individual is interacting with his environment at present but also in the past and how he has resolved his conflicts, and crises in the past. It is, therefore, feasible to take a synthetic view of the above models for explaining and understanding one's success or failure in adjustment. All the factors biological as well as social, the past as well as the present experiences, innate as well as learned patterns of behaviour, societal influence on the individual and vice-versa should be taken into consideration for understanding adjustment or maladjustment of the individual with his self or environment.

The Problem and Its Significance

RATIONALE OF THE STUDY

The fact of differences in school achievement, and the search for an explanation of those differences, is one of the most complex and, at the present time, one of the most controversial issues in education today. It has been the focus of numerous researchers and the topic of many government reports, not only in this country, but in most of the industrialized and industrializing countries of the world. Yet in spite of an impressive bibliography we are still almost as far from reaching an understanding of the actual process of school achievement as we were some decades ago.

This is not to suggest that research has been altogether inconclusive. Although a detailed review of findings would be out of place here, such factors as parents socio-economic status, family size, aspirations of both parents and children, and characteristics of the child such as ability, motivation and some personality traits have all been shown to be associated with school achievement in a wide variety of contexts. Moreover, in recent years a number of studies have attempted to assess the relative importance of these and other factors. For example the Plowden Report, England (1967) attempted to differentiate the effect of home circumstances, including the physical amenities, the number of dependent children and parents' education, from the effect of parental attitudes and from the effect of the school. Similarly Coleman (1966) in a study undertaken on behalf of the US Office of Education, looked at the relative contribution of a number of aspects of the school.

There has been a growing tendency to emphasize the non-intellectual and dynamic factors in the student's performance (Beasley, 1957, Garrett, 1949). The investigations so far undertaken have tended to focus upon a wide variety of personality traits hypothesized as factors of academic achievement. Mccandless (1961) predicted that "Poor self-concepts, implying as they often do a lack of confidence in facing and mastering the environment, might accompany deficiency in one of the most vital of the child's areas of accomplishment—his performance in school". Sinha (1966) reported that as regards their self-concepts, the low achievers tended to perceive themselves in a more favourable light."

Several investigators have found the area of adjustment to college to be of vital importance in academic achievement. As early as 1927 Corson (1927) observed that on entering the college, the freshman faces a number of new adjustment problems for which he is usually unprepared. Congdon (1943), Houston and Marzolf (1944), Hibler and Larson (1944), Carroll and Jones (1944) have all found several adjustment problems to be associated with under-achievement. Steinzor (1944), Cattell (1945), Thompson (1948) also pointed out that the over-achievers were characterized by good adjustment to school and greater awareness and responsiveness to environmental influences, Johnson (1947) hold that poor performance in college was due to unsatisfactory adjustment to college. Stormwold and Wrenn (1948) observed that a well-adjusted student exhibits high intrinsic interest in the subject matter of study, positive attitude towards the requirements of his curriculum, stability of his goals, balanced emotional life, ability to concentrate for reasonable length of time on his tasks, and ability to enjoy life in many areas. According to Anderson (1954) many under-achievers were not beset with serious personal problems. Their difficulty seems to lie in an inadequate understanding of the academic challenge coupled with an equally inadequate effort. Horrall (1957) studying students with high intelligence found that those adjudged to have good adjustment tended to be high achievers while those adjudged poorly adjusted to be low achievers. Findings of Terman and Odeon (1947), Shaw and Mccuen (1960) and

Gallenghar (1964) have emphasized that under-achievement is a continuing problem stemming from basic personality and social problems which needs treatment and care as early in the school program as is possible. French (1958) reported that lack of adjustment to college life in the freshman introduces extraneous influences on scholastic success. Christensen (1956) and Pophan and Moore (1960) observed that over-achievers significantly differ from under-achievers with regard to their adjustment to college as assessed by Borrows Inventory. Frankel (1960) found over-achievers to be more adequately adjusted to the academic situation. Rao (1967) found academic adjustment to be the greatest single factor that affected student performance.

STATEMENT OF THE PROBLEM

The distressing phenomena scholastic under-achievement and failure have been causing serious concern to educationists, guidance counsellors and educational planners for several decades as these amount to colossal wastage of resources and manpower and involve a wasteful utilization of scarce resources available for education in our country. This necessitates serious problem into the causes that underlie and factors that lead to under-achievement and failure so that means could be devised to grapple with this enormous problem. It has been asserted that apart from minimum academic requirements, the quality of scholastic performance depends upon certain personality factors.

The present scenario of educational institutions give the impression that academic achievement of the students is much stressed and development of other abilities are neglected since academically high achievers are perceived as genius in the society. When we think of the self-concept and adjustment of these students we ask ourselves that.

- Do the high achievers have positive/good self-concept and better adjustment?
- Has academic achievement and relationship with self-concept and adjustment.
- Are self-concept and adjustment positively related?

The answers to such questions are planned to be obtained empirically from this study.

OBJECTIVES

The objectives of the present study are:

1. To study the self-concept of the students in relation to sex, place of residence (i.e., rural-urban), and academic streams (i.e., Arts, Science and Commerce).

2. To study the adjustment of the students in relation to sex, place of residence and academic streams.

3. To compare the self-concept of high and low achievers.

4. To compare the adjustment patterns of high and low achievers.

5. To find out the relationship between self-concept (dimension-wise and total) and academic achievement.

6. To find out the relationship between adjustment (area-wise and total) and academic achievement.

7. To find out the relationship between self-concept (i.e., dimension wise and total) and adjustment (area-wise and total).

HYPOTHESES

In pursuance of the objectives of the study stated above, hypotheses were formulated and stated in the null form so that they could be tested statistically.

1. There is no significant sex difference in the self-concept (i.e., dimension-wise and total) of the students.

2. There is no significant difference in the self-concept (dimension-wise and total) of urban and rural students.

3. There is no significant difference in the self-concept (i.e., dimension-wise and total) of:

(a) Arts and science students;

(b) Arts and commerce students; and

(c) Science and commerce students.

4. There is no significant sex difference in the adjustment (i.e., area-wise and total) of the students.
5. There exists no significant difference in the adjustment (i.e., area-wise and total) of urban and rural students.
6. There is no significant difference in the adjustment (i.e., area-wise and total) of:

(a) Arts and science students;

(b) Arts and commerce students; and

(c) Science and commerce students.

7. There is no significant difference between the high and low achievers in their self-concept (dimension-wise and total).
8. There is no significant difference between the high and low achievers in their adjustment (area-wise and total).
9. There will be no significant relationship between self-concept (dimension-wise and total) and academic achievement of the students.
10. There will be no significant relationship between adjustment (area-wise and total) and academic achievement of the students.
11. There will no significant relationship between self-concept (dimension-wise and total) and adjustment (area-wise and total) of the students.

OPERATIONAL MEANING OF THE KEY TERMS

Difference terms have their connotations according to their place of reference. For an investigator it is almost essential to define or explain these terms which constitute the basic structure of the study and are repeatedly used in his investigation. Some of the terms are defined here as under.

Self-concept

Self-concept is a dominant element in personality pattern. Brackenridge (1965), Emmerich (1968) and Hawk (1966) viewed that the core or center of gravity of the personality pattern is the individual's concept of himself as a person as related to the world in which he lives. The quality of the individual's behaviour expressed in the way he adjusts to people and things in his environment, is related to and, to a large extent, determined by his self-concept. The structure of the self-image determines the day-to-day behaviour of the individual. Decision and reactions are determined, not by what one is, but by what one believes he is and which will tend to maintain the image intact. Rogers (1951) and his followers, while using client-centered counselling, have felt that the basic problem of many disturbed people is that their self-concept is the source of their inner discord.

Self-concept is the way one seems himself, the self of characteristics he associates with himself irrespective of particular environment in which he may be at a given moment. An individual's self-concept is a set of inferences drawn from self-observation in many different situations. These influences are descriptions of his characteristics behaviour pattern.

The self-concept is best conceived as a system of attitudes towards one-self. Just as a person, as a result of experiences forms attitudes which he organize into a self-consistent system and defends against attack even to the point of disregarding or falsifying the evidence, so the person, also as a result of his experience forms attitudes towards himself.

Self-concept has been referred by Lowe (1961) as one's attitude towards self, and by Paderson (1965) as an organized configuration, of perceptions, beliefs, feelings, attitudes and values which the individual views as part of characteristics of himself. Rogers (1951) defined self-concept as "An organized configuration of perceptions of the self which are admissible to awareness. It is compared of such elements as the perceptions of one's characteristics and abilities, the percepts and concepts of the self in relation to others and to the environment, the value qualities which are perceived as associated with experiences and objects and the goals and ideals which are perceived as having positive or negative valance". Saraswat and Gaur (1981) described self-concept as "the individual's way of looking at himself. It also signified his way of thinking, feeling and behaving".

Self-concept, as used in the present study, refers to the views of Saraswat (1984) on self-concept. It is defined as the perception of the students about their own personality qualities. Only six dimensions of self-concept (i.e., physical, social, intellectual, moral, educational and temporal) were measured in this study.

Adjustment

Man, among the living beings, has the highest capacities to adapt to new situation. Man as a social animal not only adapts to physical demands but he also adjusts to social pressures. Biologists used the terms adaptation strictly for physical demands of the environment but physiologists use the term adjustment for varying conditions of social or inter-personal relation in the society. Thus, adjustment may be seen as reaction to the demands and pressures of social environment imposed upon the individual. Good (1959) said that adjustment is the process of finding and adopting modes of behaviour suitable to the environment or the changes in the environment.

Adjustment in this study is considered as that "What Sinha and Singh's (1993) adjustment inventory measures."

Academic Achievement

According to Baron and Bernard (1962) the concept of achievement involves the interaction of three factors, namely, aptitude for learning, readiness for learning and opportunity for learning. Achievement in education, precisely speaking, implies one's knowledge, understanding or skills etc. in specified subject or a group of subjects.

According to Wiley and Andrew (1955) one of the main purposes of measuring the achievement of pupils is to ascertain the degree to which the educational objectives of the school are being realized. The results of the measurement of achievement, taken at intervals over a period of years, provide a continuous means of evaluating the students growth and help to determine the effectiveness of the curriculum in meeting the individual needs. The other purpose served by achievement measurement, on the basis of standardized tests are diagnosis and prediction tests.

Generally, teachers use marks to record their judgement about the students level of academic achievement. These marks are generally based on the internal and external examinations. The marks represent estimates of the proficiency possessed by the student in school subjects. Some studies despite criticism, support the view point that the marks obtained or the academic level attained on the basis of these examinations continue to be fairly stable.

In the present study, academic achievement is operationally defined as the total marks secured by the subjects in the Annual H.S.C. Examination 1999 conducted by the Board of Secondary Education Orissa.

DELIMITATIONS

The scope of the study has been limited to its area, method, sampling, tools and techniques proposed for the study. The study has been delimited in the following ways.

(i) The study is confined to three major variables (i.e., self-concept, adjustment and academic achievement). Variables selected for the study are related to the two domains, namely affective (self-concept and adjustment) and cognitive (academic achievement) respectively. Their presence in students and their relationship with each other

is not an easy task to measure. Further academic achievement is measured in terms of percentage of marks obtained in the Annual H.S.C. Examination 1999 conducted by B.S.E. Orissa.

(ii) Only six dimensions of self-concept and three areas of adjustment have been taken in this study.

(iii) The study has been conducted on 600 students of +2 stage (i.e., 1st year only)

(iv) The sample for the study was drawn only from undivided Koraput District of Orissa.

(v) The present study is restricted to the high achievers and low achievers. Average students have not been considered in the study.

(vi) Exclusion of average students has reduced the sample size which has been 286 (i.e., High Achievers N = 144 and Low Achievers N = 142) for final analysis.

(vii) A descriptive research method has been used in the present study.

(viii) The statistical techniques like t-test, product moment correlation were employed to analyse data.

3

Review of Related Literature

Practically all-human knowledge can be found in books and libraries. Unlike other animals that must start a new with each generation man builds upon the accumulated and recorded knowledge of the past.

The review of related studies is essential for several reasons. It helps in identifying the unanswered questions in the concerned field on the one hand and in locating the specific issues which require immediate and pointed attack by the investigator on the other.

The review of related literature works as a guide post not only with regards to quantum of work done in that field but also enables us to perceive the gap in the concerned field of research. It is highly essential for a researcher to make a comprehensive survey of what has already been done in the related areas. The purpose of the review of literature is to build up the context and background of research as well as to provide a basis for formulation of the hypotheses. Since a good research is based upon everything that is known in the area of research, the review of research provides to this effect.

The review of literature is an exacting task calling for a deep insight and clear perspective of the over all field. The time spent in it invariably accounts for a wise investment. It invariably minimizes wasted efforts. The review of literature promotes greater understanding of the problem and its crucial aspects and ensures avoidance of unnecessary duplication. For progress to occur, it is essential that new work be based and built on what has already been accomplished. In this context, Mouly (1964) states, "Survey of related literature avoids the risk of duplication, provides theories, ideas, explanations or hypotheses valuable in formulating the problem and contributes to the general scholarship of the investigator.

In the present research the investigator has scanned most of the relevant and reported studies done in India and abroad in the field of self-concept, adjustment and achievement pertaining not only to the secondary students, but also the pupils and other functionaries associated with the process of education. The present chapter provides a thumb-nail account of such studies their ambit and outcomes.

The available researches, which are directly and indirectly related to the present study have been conveniently classified under three main headings.

Studies on Self-Concept

1. *Comparative studies*
2. *Self-concept and Achievement*
3. *Self-concept and other variables*

Studies on Adjustment

1. *Comparative studies*
2. *Adjustment and Achievement*
3. *Adjustment and other variables*

Studies on Self-Concept, Adjustment and Achievement

STUDIES ON SELF-CONCEPT

The idea of self-concept was originally proposed by Lecky (1945) and adopted by Rogers (1951) as the keystone of his system of non-directive counselling. This concept is of major importance in education, particularly, in the more personal aspects of motivation, attitudes, character formation and adjustment which, in turn, are the foundation upon which school and out of school success must rest.

Self-concept as an area of research has attracted the attention of many scholars, as a result of which a large number of studies have been undertaken.

In some studies attempts have been made to compare the subjects across their sex, caste, residence, academic stream and culture etc. Some studies have been directed to find out the relationship between self-concept and other variables. All such studies have been presented below.

1. Comparative Studies

Self-concept in an individual develops though learning attitudes, school/colleges environment, social factors and his community background. These and other variables play important role in the development of self-concept. Moreover, it is an acquired or learned process through the influence of several variables. A number of researches are available in this field.

A study entitled, "Change in self-concepts in relation to perception of others" by Kipins (1961) revealed that perception of others, which are used as a basis for comprehension should be an important determinant of self-evaluation. It was found that subjects perceived smaller differences between themselves and their best friends that that between themselves and a less liked room-mate. Subjects, who perceived their best friends to be relatively unlike themselves, changed their self-evaluation more in a six weeks time interval than did subjects who perceived their best friends to be like themselves. The subjects change their self-evaluation during the six weeks time interval so that they perceived smaller differences between themselves and their best friends.

Aniloff (1977) found that the students who selected academic programme had more positive self-concepts and higher occupational expectations than the students whom selected business programme.

On the basis of self-concept scores, Seaward (1977) reported that the cooperative vocational office-training students were significantly higher than the intensive business-training students. Regular business education students demonstrated significantly higher scores than the intensive business training students but not significantly different from cooperative vocational students.

Drlington (1978) reported that there was no positive change in the self-concept of elementary education majors as a result of physical education clinical experience.

In a comparative study Lall (1978) found that there was no significant difference in the self-concept of Mckinney Job corps Graduates and Non-Job Corps Graduates.

M.C. Gough (1978) found in a comparative study that there was no significant difference between non-disadvantaged and disadvantages students when the self-concept was measured by TSCS.

Silverman (1978) reported that there were no significant difference among urban, sub-urban and rural learning disables groups on the total self-concept scores. The urban disabled and urban non-disabled groups were significantly higher than the norming groups.

Bhadauria (1980) Found that

(i) the overall means score of the gifted students was significantly higher than that of the non-gifted students; (ii) gifted students had significantly higher positive aspects of self-concept, (iii) they showed significantly higher degree of confidence, (iv) the achievement scores were also higher, (v) the gifted students had significantly higher negative aspect of self-concept, (vi) they exhibited significantly higher degree of withdrawal, inferiority feelings and emotional instability than the gifted students.

The study of Bharathi (1984) revealed the following findings:

1. older age group subjects perceived themselves as being less able, less aspiring for greater ability and showed more dissatisfaction with their ability,

2. no age differences were found in self-concept with respect to adjustment,
3. no significant age differences were found in the personal social orientation aspect of self-concept in the real self-concept,
4. in the masculinity-feminity aspect of self-concept, age differences were not significant,
5. at different age levels, different self-concept measures were found to be related with n-achievement,
6. in the ability aspect on self-concept on sex differences were observed,
7. girls perceived themselves better adjusted and also aspired to be better adjusted than boys,
8. boys perceived themselves to be more personally oriented than girls and they also aspired to be more personally oriented,
9. boys perceived themselves to be more masculine and also would like to be more masculine as compared to girls,
10. girls were more dissatisfied with their perceived self then boys,
11. low socio-economic status subjects perceived themselves less adjusted and felt greater dissatisfaction with themselves in this aspect,
12. low socio-economic status subjects wanted to be more socially oriented as compared to high and middle SES subjects,
13. the self-concept of ability was not affected by socio-economic status,
14. the influence of the age variable on the masculinity feminity aspect of self-concept was different in different SES groups.

15. middle SES groups showed greater satisfaction with self in general.

Harper (1990) investigated the inferred (teacher report) and professed (self report) self-concept-as-learner scores of 400 sixth, seventh and eighth grade gifted and average students in two middle schools in North Carolina. Data were collected from randomly selected classes of average and gifted students by using two forms of the Florida Key, (Purkey, Cage and Graves, 1973) an instrument designed to measure student self-concept-as-learner. Five hypotheses and twelve corollary hypotheses were tested.

Results of the study indicated significantly and progressively lower combined scores for 7th and 8th grade students when compared with those of 6th grade students. The same results were found when inferred and professed scores were considered separately.

The study showed significantly higher group scores at all three grade levels for academically gifted (AG) students when compared with average (AV) students. The results were the same when inferred and professed SCAL measures were combined and considered separately.

Other results of the study indicated significant differences in-group scores between male and female students across 6th, 7th, and 8th grade levels. Females scored higher than males at all three grade levels when inferred and professed scores were considered separately and when they were combined.

Significant changes were discovered in professed scores from fall to spring with spring scores being significantly lower. There were no significant differences in inferred scores from fall to spring.

No significant differences were found between inferred and professed scores for the fall testing. However, gifted students inferred and professed scores for spring were significantly different, with professed scores being lower than inferred scores.

The major conclusion of this study is that there is a significant and progressive decline of self concept-as-learner of students from 6th to 8th grade and over a five-month period. This finding holds true for both gifted and average students, male and female, and is based on both professed and inferred measures.

Martel (1990) carried out of study to examine the effects of sex, self-concept traits and self-concept grouping on the academic performances of black middle school students. The researcher of this study were more specifically concerned with the effect of the self-concept (high, average and low) on students in six academic areas of their preparation as measured by the Metropolitan Achievement Test. These academic areas were vocabulary, reading, mathematics, science, language, arts and social science.

A series of single factor designs was employed in this study. Two hundred twenty four (224) middle school students from four middle schools were randomly selected to participate in this survey.

The data were collected by administering the Piers-Harris children's Self-Concept Scale and the Metropolitan Achievement Test to the student. The data analysis for the study was obtained through the application of the one-way Analysis of Variance and Scheffe's post-hoc test.

The following conclusions were drawn from this study.

1. Black middle school students with high self-concepts scored significantly higher on the vocabulary section of the Metropolitan Achievement Test than did those school students with average self-concept.

2. Black middle school students with high self-concepts did significantly higher on the total Metropolitan Achievement Test that did those black middle school students with low self-concepts.

3. Male and female black middle school students obtained similar scores on the vocabulary, reading,

mathematics, science, language, arts and social sections of the Metropolitan Achievement Test.

4. The academic performance of black middle school students on the Metropolitan Achievement Test were influenced by their self-concept grouping traits.

Callis (1991) made an attempt to test the effectiveness of a programme designed to improve the self-concept of youngsters (mean age = 13.67 years) who participated in an experimental design study which compared results on measures prior to and after a 10 week coping skill group. Children were randomly assigned to treatment and control conditions before administration of the Coopersmith Self-Esteem Inventory, a “Significant other” rating scale, and behaviour observations of center staff. The control group worked on academic study skill while the Treatment group dealth with issues presumed to related to self-concept. At the conclusion of the 10 week course, data were again collect on the measures.

It was hypothesized that Treatment groups would show greater improvements on the variables. This predication was not supported since both group actually scored lower in the post-test circumstances for self-concept and behaviour observations. Ratings by significant others, however, did prove to be distinguishing with the Treatment groups posting a 4.64 point gain on the 55 point instrument developed for this study. Behaviour observations showed no significant distinctions. Tests for differences in age and gender also resulted in no major differences except for post-test observation scores where females scored significantly higher.

Martin (1991) studies the role of self-concept and locus of control with respect to the academic achievement of college students with learning disabilities. Pre-college students with learning disabilities have consistently been shown to have a proper academic self-concept and more external locus of control than their non-learning disabled peers. Since both of these traits are negatively correlated with academic achievement, this study sought to determine if this pattern is present in a sample of college students with learning disabilities. In addition, self-concept and locus of control were examined to see the relationship between these constructs and the student's grade point average, gender, age and socio-economic status.

Results of the study indicated that college students with learning disabilities continue to demonstrate significantly proper academic self-concepts (on verbal, math, and general academic scales) than non-learning disabled students.

However, their attributional patterns differed from that found in research on pre-college students with learning disabilities. They were less likely to use external causes, such as task difficulty or luck, to explain their success or failure. It appears that the college learning disabled population may differ from the pre-college population primary along this dimension. Female students with learning disabilities were much more likely to attribute their success (or failure) to their ability (or lack of ability) than to their effort. No other gender, age, or socio-economic status differences were noted. Finally, a regression analysis indicated that academic self-concept best explained the learning disabled student's grade point average, non-academic self-concept was the second most significant predictor, and more powerful than any of the locus of control factors.

Arcangelo (1992) examined and compared the self-perceptions of interpersonal relationship and self concepts of a group of 40 learning disabled (LD) adults and 41 non-learning (non-LD) disabled adults (age 19-0 through 28-0). All subjects in the study had attended the same public school. Both groups were comparable in race, age, sex, and socio-economic status (SES). All LD subjects were classified by the public school district and received special education services as LD students. The non-LD subjects attended regular education classes.

Subjects were mailed and Social Adjustment Scale (SAS-SR, Weissman and Bothwell, 1976), the Tennessee Self-Concept Scale (TSS: Fitts and Roid, 1988) and a demographic questionnaire. Multiple Regression and Multivariate Analysis of Variance indicated on significant differences between the two groups on SAS-SR total or subscales scores or TSS total or subtest score.

Stepwise Multiple Regression procedures indicated that achievement and intelligence test score accounted for most variance (96%) in SAS-SR. Total scores where as intelligence test scores and socio-economic status accounted for most variance (58%) in TSS total scores. Of particular interest is the fact that despite significant group differences, 20% of the LD sample obtained, TSS scores falling within a clinically low range of self-concept (Total T-Scores <40 on the TSS). Results are discussed in terms of implications for future research in the study of LD adults.

Bissa, Singh and Helode (1993) compared the self-concept of blind and normal students.

It was found that blind subjects were at par with the normal subjects on all dimensions of self-concept. Blind and normal students showed similar self-concept on all six dimensions.

Agarwal (1994) studied the relationship between sex and general self-concept in grade IX students. He found that the mean score of girls was greater than those of boys in the case of identity, self-satisfaction, behaviour, physical, moral-ethical, personal, self-criticism, total self-concept and its instability dimension. In the remaining two cases (family and social self), the values for the two sexes were almost identical. The study also found the superiority of girls over boys in their role specific self-concept.

2. Self-Concept and Achievement

Many psychologists and educationists have attempted to explain the achievement behaviour in terms of the concepts which the school pupils develop about themselves and the world around. Raimy (1948) attached a perceptual frame of reference to the behaviour. He said that each individual perception of himself is of ultimate psychological significance in organized behaviour. We act in accordance with our perceptions.

A similar theory has been sponsored by Jersild (1952) who holds that "when a person resists learning that may be beneficial to him, he, is, in effect, trying to protect or to shield an unhealthy condition. But, more broadly speaking, he is not actually protecting something unhealthy as such: he is trying to safeguard his picture of himself, hisself, concept develops the illusions concerning himself which he has built and which give him much trouble."

Combs (1958) emphasized that inadequate perception of self-results inadequate performance and failures are largely due to unfortunate attitudes towards educational tasks.

Combs and Snygg (1959) stated that the behaviour should be understood as growing out of the individual subjects frame of reference as, "what a person thinks and how he behaves are largely determined by the concepts he holds about himself and his abilities."

Hatfield (1961) also has expressed a similar view in the following words.

"Adequately functioning personalities see themselves in essentially positive way. They assume that they are persons that are liked, wanted and loved for their own sake. They become self-confident, self-assured, self-reliant members of society. Self-depreciation results in a falling of effective functioning."

An attempt was made by Deo and Sharma (1970) to find out the relationship between self-concept and school achievement. Seven hundred students (362 males and 338 females) selected randomly from final year of thirteen higher secondary schools taken on random basis from four States of the Indian Union acted as subjects. The Self-concept Inventory (Sharma 1967) was administered to 700 students in small batched of 15 to 20 to obtain Self-concept Scores. Achievement scores were taken from the marks obtained by all the Ss in the Punjab University Higher Secondary

Examination, 1967. The data were processed to find out whether mean achievement scores of five Self-concept groups differed significantly from each other or not. It was observed that 'Middle' scored higher in achievement than the extreme Self-concept groups. The subjects with 'low' Self-concept and 'high' Self-concept differed significantly at 0.01 level from the middle group, but did not differ significantly from each other. Further, it was observed that even though extreme Self-concept groups did not differ significantly from each other. Ss with high positive Self-concept achieved higher than the Ss with high negative Self-concept. The value of *r* between Self-concept Scores and achievement scores was found to be 0.037, which suggests a curvilinear relationship between Self-concept and school achievement.

Rowand (1989) made an attempt to explore the relationship among gifted achieving and underachieving adolescents perceptions of academic ability, global self-concept, perception of school performance, intelligence and achievement. The subjects of this study were ninth grade gifted adolescents (N = 69) enrolled in seven schools in a large country in a southern state located in the southeastern region of the United States. All subjects had been staffed into the country-gifted program. Criteria for admission included teacher recommendation and an IQ score of 130 on the WISC-R or 132 on the Stanford Binet.

Under-achievers were defined as students who hade an IQ scores of 130 or above and a mean GPA of 2.5 or below. Achievers were defined as those students with an IQ of 130 or above and a mean GPA of 3.5 or above.

Perceptions of academic ability and self-concept were measured by the Harter Self-Perception Profile for Adolescents (1988) and the Gough Adjective Checklist (1983) Self-Confidence Scale.

It was hypothesized that achievers would have higher perceptions of ability and self-concept than underachievers. Additionally, it was hypothesized that males would perceive themselves to be more intelligent than females and would also have better self-concepts.

All hypotheses were tested utilizing a 2 × 2 analysis of variance. The SAS-PC computer programme was used for analysis. The dependent variables were the perception of academic ability and self-concept scores on the Harter Scale and the self-concept score on the Gough Adjective Checklist.

The results of 2 × 2 analysis of variance and independent t-test found that gifted achievers had higher perceptions of academic ability and school performance ability than gifted underachievers. Males had higher perceptions of intelligence than females as well as lower competence importance discrepancy scores, which reflected positive male self-concept.

There was a significant group by gender interaction among groups on self-concept in that achieving males had the highest self-concept and achieving females had the lowest, and underachieving males and females were almost identical.

Malarczyk (1990) investigated the relationship between scholastic performance and self-concept of grade ten military dependents and three selected variables in the military environment.

The sample consisted of 119 tenth-grade students from seven Canadian military bases: Six in Canand and one Defence base in Germany. Criterion variables were reading comprehension mathematics achievement, written expression and self-concept. Predictor variables were geographic mobility, father absence due to assignment, and military status. The sample was stratified by gender for data analysis.

The performance of the research sample on the criterion variables was compared with the published norms through construction confidence intervals. Relationship between criterion and predictor variables were examined through partial correlations after controlling for the influence of cognitive ability. Multiple regression analysis were used to examine the relationship between the predictor variables and each criterion variables for each gender group. Bonferroni adjustment was used to guard against experiment-wise error.

The research sample was found to be similar to the norming samples of instruments used for data-collection, except for mathematics and cognitive ability. There was no support for significant relationships between the environmental variables and the criterion variables. None of the bivariate correlations between the environmental and the criterion variables was statistically significant after Bonferroni adjustment for the control of Type 1 error. As well, none of the multiple regression analysis was statistically significant at the. 0125 alpha levels. However, the military environmental factors investigated in this study did not appear to be detrimental to the adolescent's school achievement and self-concept. It is speculated that cognitive ability may be a mediating variable in the relationship of military environmental variables and performance in school subjects.

Moulton (1990) examined the relationship between self-concept, academic achievement and behavioural patterns of an experimental group of seventh grade-at-risk students. Specifically, this experimental study was designed to analyze the impact for a social skills intervention on the self-concept of those determined to be at-risk. Changes in self-concept were comparing to corresponding changes in academic achievement and behavioral performance.

A randomized could group pretest-post-test design was used in this experimental study. An experimental placebo and control group were randomly selected from 90 seventh grade at-risk students. The experimental group received a social skill intervention, the placebo group received a study hall and the control group received no direct attention during the 18-week experimental period.

The primary instrument for measuring the impact of the social skills intervention on self-concept was the Piers-Harris children's self-concept scale. A one-way analysis of covariance was used to examine the dependent variable of self-concept.

Academic achievement and behaviour were analysed on the basis of the average means score of the first and second semester academic grade point average, disciplinary referrals, attendance and marks in citizenship and effort. In each analysis of covariance, the pre-assessment score was used as the covariate and the post-test assessment score as the criterion. A .05 level of probability as selected as the critical value for establishing statistical significance.

A analysis of the data obtained in the study revealed there were no statistically significant changes in the self-concept, academic achievement and behavioural performance of the experimental, palacebo and control groups of seventh grade at-risk students following on 18-weeks treatment of the experimental group with a social skills intervention.

Barry (1991) also examined the relationship among specific domains of self-concept and domains of academic achievement for learning disabled children. Subjects were 109 intermediate grade students attending public schools in Indiana. All subjects had been classified by their school districts as LD and were currently receiving resources room services. Additionally, the relationship between actual self-concepts scores and inferred self-concept scores was explored by asking resource room teachers to complete the Self-Description Questionnnaire-1 (SD. Q-1) as they believed each of their students would respond.

The SD Q-1 was administered to assess the domains of self-concept, while achievement in reading, mathematics, and written language was operationalized as scores on the Woodcock-Johnson Psycho-Educational Battery Test of Achievement (WJPB). Ability scores from the Wechsier Intelligence Scale for Children Revised (WISC-R) and WJPB achievement scores were collected from student's school files.

Pearson correlation coefficients were computed to investigate the relationship among individual variables. Only one significant correlation ($P < .01$) was found between domains of self-concept and domains of academic achievement. The Low correlation (–.07) existed between reading self-concept and achievement in Written language. Interestingly, every inter-corelation among the SD Q-1 domain was significant calling into question the purported factor structure of he SD Q-1 with this LD population.

A canonical correlation analysis was used to investigate at the associations among multiple variables, such as ability, self-concept domains and achievement domains. Since the link between ability and achievements has been supported in the literature, the intent of this analysis was to investigate the extent that self-concept contributed to achievement. Results of this analysis also suggested a significant relationship between ability and achievement; however, above and beyond ability, knowledge of self-concept scores did not aid to the relationship with achievement.

In addition to exploring the association among domains of self-concept and domains of achievement, this study also examined the relationship between actual and inferred self-concept scores. Results of a canonical correlation analysis supported a significant relationship between actual self-concept and inferred self-concept scores. It appeared that resource room teachers were accurately able to infer the self-concepts of their LD students. This agreement between self-report and teacher report of self-concept is consistent with previous research.

In conclusion, the present investigation did not provide support for a relationship between domains of self-concept and academic achievement with this LD sample. The implications for results are discussed along with suggestions of further research in this area.

The investigation made by James (1991) tried to explore the extent to which non-cognitive variables were related to the academic achievement of pre-dominantly low achieving Black suburban high school students. Specially, Perceived Support from Family (PSFAM), School (PSSCH), and Peers (PSPEER) were considered along with general Self-concept (SC) and Self-concept of Academic Ability (SCA). Along with Black students, others were included in the sample in order to explore whether these variables related differently to the academic achievement of students of different races.

For Black students, the variable which significantly correlated with GPA were SCA (r = .26, p < .05) explaining 6.85 of variance, and PSFAM (r = –.20, P < .05) explaning 4% of variance SCA and PSFAM together, were also significant. (R = .35, P <. 005) explaining 12.1% of variance in GPA of Black Students. Intragroup analysis, however, revealed the heterogeneity of the Black students. SCA was significantly related to the GPA of Black students attending a predominately Black school (r = .56, p < .01), explaning 31% of variance, and the GPA of Black Females (r = .36, p = .004) explaining 13% of variance PSFAM was significantly inversely related to GPA for Black females (r = –.31, p = .011) explaining 9.6% of variance and for Black students in the enrichment program (r = –.38, p = .024), explaining 14.4% of variance. For White students, the variables which significantly related to GPA were SCA (r = .62, p < .01) explaining 38.4% of variance.

Rangappa (1994) studied the effect of self-concept on achievement in mathematics. It was found that there was a significant difference in achievement of the students of class VII in mathematics belonging to high, normal and low self-concept groups. The students of class VII belonging to high self-concept group performed better in mathematics than the students belonging to normal self-concept group. There was a high significant difference of achievement between high and low self-concept groups. Students of class VII belonging to high self-concept group performed better in mathematics than the students belonging to low self-concept group. The students of class VII belonging to normal self-concept group performed better in mathematics than the students belonging to low self-concept group.

Maikhuri and Panda (1997) studied the self-concept of adolescents in relations to their academic achievement. The tools used to collect the data included Self-Concept Inventory by Deo. The collected data were treated with means, SD and 't' test.

It was found that (1) academic achievement and self-concept were not significantly related, (2) no significant difference was found between achievement of adolescents belonging to high and low self-concept.

Shah (1988) conducted to study on the relationship of self-concept to academic achievement of Secondary School pupils. The major objectives of the study were:

(i) to find out the relationship between SC and academic achievement,

(ii) to find out whether girls as a group indicated higher positive self-concept, and

(iii) to see whether there was any significant difference in the SC of pupils of Grades IX and X. It was found that

(a) there was no significant sex difference in self-concept at grade IX while the same at grade X was significant,

(b) the girls as a group did not indicate higher positive self-concepts,

(c) there was no significant difference between the mean scores on the self-concept of pupils studying in grade IX and X.

(d) the relationship between self-concept and academic achievement was significantly positive and linear.

3. Self-Concept and other Variables

Attempts have also been made by the researcher to explain the behaviour in terms of the concepts which the children develop about themselves and the world around in relation to some other variables. Some of the important studies are given below.

Ramkumar (1979) found that (i) the community of students was found to be an important contributory factor for actual self-concept, (ii) the area of residence and the size of the family did not contribute to acute self-concept, (iii) the extreme group showed lower intelligence scores than the normal group, (iv) personal and social adjustment scores of the extreme group were significantly lower than those of the normal group. Similarly the mean withdrawing tendency score of the extreme group was lower than that of the normal group, (v) the extreme group had significantly higher means scores than the normal group on four value areas religious, political, aesthetical and theoretical. The extreme group had significantly lower scores in social values and exhibited no difference in economic values, (vi) a very high percentage of the backward community girls was found to have acute self-concept.

Saxena (1981) reported that the socio-economic status had the most significant effects on self-concept, study habit and school attitude of different division as well as failures of high school. Rural culture promoted better study habits and achievement level because the rural students did not involve themselves in bad practices prevalent in an urban area. It was interesting to note that the first order interaction between socio-economic status and cultural setting had no significant effect on self-concept, study habit and school attitude. Also the second order interaction among scholastic achievement, socio-economic status and cultural setting had no significant effect on self-concept, study habit and school attitude.

Panwar (1986) concluded that (1) academic achievement had significant effect on self-concept, (2) home background had significant effect on self-concept, and (3) school background had significant effect on self-concept.

An attempt was made by Campbell (1990) to compare the self-concept and locus of control of specific learning disabled elementary students with non-disabled elementary students. Tenure of the specific learning-disabled students in a special education program and its relationship to each of the constructs were investigated. The sample for the study was comprised of 100 students (50 specific learning disabled students and 50 nondiasbled) students) ranging in age from

10 to 14 years of age. Tenure of the specific learning disables students in a special education programme ranged from 1 to 89 months. Two instruments were administered to the students, the Piers-Harris children's self-concept scale and the Nowicki-Strickland Internal-External Locus of control scale.

The data were analyzed using independent *t*-tests, Pearson's product-moment correlation's, and stepwise multiple regression procedures. The .05 level of significance served as the basis of rejecting a null hypothesis. Finding indicate that there are significant differences between the specific learning disabled students and non-disabled students on global self-concept and with the exception of anxiety self-concept, all components of self-concept. Specific learning disabled students also exhibited a more external locus of control that the no disabled students did. Tenure of specific learning disables students in a special education programme has no relationship to either construct.

From the finding of the study the following conclusions may be made. Specific learning disables students perceived themselves more negatively than non-diasbled students. Lower self-concept scores were associated with more external locus of control scores. Finally there was a need for additional emphasis on the development of a positive self-concept and a more internal locus of control for specific learning disabled students.

The study of Grzegorek (1990) was concerned with the question of whether self-concept is a variable, which contributes significantly to the presence of obesity in adult, pre-menopausal, white females. The main issue examined was whether there is a significant difference in self-concept between obese women and non-obese women. The second issue examined was whether there is a significant difference in self-concept between obese women who seek help for weight reduction and those obese women who have never sought help for weight reduction.

The above variables were assessed when comparing the following three groups. (1) 49 obese woman who have never sought help for weight reduction; (2) 34 obese women who were seeking help for weight reduction via participation in a group weight-loss program (weight watchers or Tops), and (3) 49 nonobese women with no history of obesity. The women ranged in age from 26 to 46 years of age, and responded to a newspaper advertisement-requesting participants for weight-reduction research.

The 132 participants were weighed, had their body frame sizes determined, and had their heights measured. The participants were then administered the Tennessee Self-Concept Scale (TSCS). An analysis of variance was performed comparing the TSCS scores of all the obese participants to those scores of all of the nonobese participants. Additionally, an analysis of variance was done which compared the TSCS scores of the group of obese women who sought help for weight reduction with the TSCS scores of those obese women who have never sought help.

The results of the investigation indicated that there was no significant difference in self-concept scores between obese women and nonobese women. Also, no significant difference in self-concept scores was found between obese women who sought help for weight reduction and those obese women who have never sought help for weight reduction.

The study of Shaffer (1990) was designed to determine if there was a significant difference between the self-concepts of moderate to severely and profoundly hearing impaired students who were partially or fully mainstreamed into the regular elementary or secondary schools. The students' self-concept was examined from their own perspective on the Piers-Harris children's self-Concept Scale and from the classroom teachers' perspective on the Meadon-Kendall Social-Emotional Assessment Inventory for Hearing-Impaired students. Fully mainstreamed was defined as less than five hours of direct service a week. Partially mainstreamed was more than five hours of direct service. Tutor interpreter hours were non-included in these hours.

Forty-eight students and their regular classroom teachers participated. The students all had hearing parents and not other handicapping conditions. Their hearing losses were discovered before three. They were in their current placement for two years.

A three-way analysis of variance was used to determine if there was interaction among the independent variables, mainstreaming, hearing loss, and level in school, for the two dependent variables, the self-concept results on the Piers-Harris and Meadow-Kendall. A significant interaction occurred between the amount of mainstreaming and the degree of hearing loss on the Piers-Harris. Post hoc analysis revealed that this interaction was significant for the fully mainstreamed profoundly hearing-impaired students. Their self-concept scores were significantly lower than the partially mainstreamed profoundly hearing-impaired students and lower than either the partially or fully mainstreamed students with moderate to – severe hearing losses. The main effect, level in school, also reached significance. Elementary children had higher self-concept scores on the Piers-Harris than secondary children.

None of the interactions or main effects reached significance on the Meadow - Kendall. Correlation coefficients revealed no relationship between the Piers-Harris and the Meadow-Kendall.

These results suggest that profoundly hearing-impaired students' self-concept may be negatively impacted by mainstreaming with only a minimum of direct services and few students like them. Students with moderate to severe losses demonstrated higher self-concepts when they were more fully mainstreamed with some direct services. The low correlation between teachers' and students' ratings suggest that regular classroom teachers may not be fully aware of the influence of hearing loss on the students self-concept.

Bell (1991) examined the relationship among student's self-attributions for social and academic success and failure, dimensions of self-concept and social functioning. Social attributions were measured using the Students' Social Attribution Scale (SSAS) which was developed for this study.

The SSAS is a measure of effort, ability and external attributions for social success and failure in the school setting. Cronbach's alpha, item-sub scale correlations and test-retest reliability co-efficient provided evidence that the scale is psychometrically sound; factor analyses provided evidence for a predicted six-factor structure.

Academic attributions were assessed using the Sydney Attribution Scale (SAS), a scale developed in Australia, but validated for use with American students from data collected in this study; self-concept was assessed using the Self-Description Questionnaire; (SDQ) social functioning was assessed using the Social Skills Rating System (SSRS); finally, academic achievement was assessed using the comprehensive Test of Basic Skills (STBS/4). The instruments were administered to 237 4th and 5th graders according to scripted directions.

Generally, social, reading, and math success attributed to ability and effort were significantly positively related to predicted dimensions of self-concept (SDQ scores) and to social behaviour (SSRS) and academic achievement (CTBS/4 scores). For example, children who highly endorsed effort as a cause for making friends were more likely to have higher social self-concepts and social skills scores than were children who less highly endorsed effort as a cause for friend making. Generally, social, reading, and math failure attributed to ability and effort were significantly negatively related to predicted dimensions of self-concept and to performance.

Although attributions, self-concept and (social and academic) performance may causally influence each other in a reciprocal manner, results from a path analysis provided support for the following causal paths: (1) attributions for social success and failure outcomes lead to social self-concept, which in turn leads to social functioning, and similarly. (2) attributions for academic success and failure outcomes lead to academic self-concept, which in turn leads to academic achievement.

Results provided evidence that attributions were related to self-concept and social and academic performance. With further development the SSAS and the SAS may be used to assess social and academic attributions to plan school-based interventions.

The study of Valdiviesco (1991) investigated the effects of school racial composition, minority curriculum offerings, and academic programmed enrollment on the self-concept, locus of control, Grades, and aspirations of Puerto Rican students. The sample consisted of 289 Puerto Rican high school senior drawn from 111 schools in the nationally representative high school and beyond survey.

The analysis was conducted in two stages. In the first stage, five theoretically important variables were used in regression analysis to account for as much variance of the dependent variables as possible, before preparing the resultant residual scores on the dependent variables for the second stage. The control variables were family, socio-economic status, general, ability, racial identification, English language proficiency, and college preparatory program enrollment.

In the second stage, analyses of variance (ANOVAs) were used to discover whether the observed differences in the means of the groups of students in schools that differed on the independent (contextual) variables could be reasonably attributed to true differences between the groups. Three of the original 14 hypotheses were found to be statistically significant: percentage of a school's 12 grade enrolled in academic programme is related positively to both self-concept and aspirations, and the number of minority curriculum offerings by a school is related negatively to locus of control.

Some conclusions suggested by the findings. First, Puerto Rican self-concept and aspirations can be affected positively by school policies that do not track students and that offer an academic curriculum. Second, a contextual variable has more explanatory power if it reflects school organization that affects how adults and students related to each other. Contextual variable based on school policies that are central to the organization of schooling, or that are simply based on student background characteristics, explain negligible amounts of variability in school outcomes. Finally, minority curriculum offerings are not related to an increase in self-concept but may unintentionally increase external locus of control for Puerto Rican students.

In a study of higher secondary school students achievement in Zoology in relation to anxiety, achievement—motivation and self-concept Minnalkodi (1997) found that (i) there was a significant difference between boys and girls on achievement scores, achievement-motivation, but not on anxiety or self-concept; (ii) the rural and urban students didn't differ on their achievement, but on anxiety, achievement-motivation and self-concept, they differed significantly, (iii) the government and private school students differed significantly on their achievement, anxiety, while they did not differ on achievement-motivation and self-concept scores; (iv) as regards the educational levels of parents, children who belonged to different educational levels differed significantly on their achievement, but not anxiety achievement-motivation and self-concept; (v) differing occupational status did not affect the achievement, anxiety, achievement-motivation, and self-concept of students; (vi) differing income levels of parents did affect the achievement levels of students and anxiety but not achievement-motivation and self-concept; (vii) there was a significant positive relationship among achievement scores, achievement-motivation, and self-concept of students.

STUDIES ON ADJUSTMENT

People react to their personal conflicts and frustrations and to the demands of the environment in divergent way. These reactions, according to Schneiders (1955) are known as 'pattern of adjustment'. Such an approach has to do with the kind of response that a person makes to whatever problems, difficulties or demands he encounters. Another approach complementary to this is concerned with the study of human adjustment from the standpoint of the situational context of the response. This involves finding out how does the person responds to his home to school, to himself and to his social environment.

Innumerable researches have been carried out in the field of adjustment both in India and abroad. Many of them have been concerned with variables such as scholastic achievement, intelligence, self-concept, level of aspiration etc. All these studies are given below.

1. Comparative Studies

Various studies comparing different groups on adjustment have been carried out Parween (1955) made an attempt to study the adjustment of disadvantaged students. The main objective of the study was to decide whether there was a distinct adjustment patterns among the deprived and disadvantages groups. For this study the Sample comprises 200 schools going students of whom 100 belonged to disadvantaged families and 100 belonged to advantaged families. Adjustment Inventory of A.K.P. Sinha and R.P. Singh was used to collect the data. The collected data were treated with mean and *'t'* ratio. He found that the advantage and the disadvantaged groups differed significantly on social, emotional and educational areas and such differences were in favour of the advantaged groups. On all the three areas, the disadvantaged groups showed unsatisfactory level of adjustments too.

The study of Nomani (1965) indicated that

1. There was no significant difference in the adjustment of males and females.
2. No significant difference was found in the adjustment of Ranchi and Sindega samples.
3. The male and female samples did not significantly differ in different areas of adjustment
4. A significant difference was found in health adjustment of Ranchi and Sindega samples. Sindega samples showed a poor adjustment.

5. College boys were superior to the school-boys in respect of family adjustments.

6. Ranchi school students tended to have better health adjustments than Sindega school students. But the difference was statistically not significant.

7. Social adjustment in general was not satisfactory.

Pandey (1970) found that: *(i)* Supernormal and normal did not differ in home, health and emotional adjustments, (ii) Normal adolescents of 15, 17 and 18 years had significant superiority over supernormal adolescents of the same ages with regards to social adjustment, (iii) Normal adolescents had superiority over supernormal adolescents in the case of social values.

Asha (1978) studied the adjustment patterns of creative children of secondary schools. The study attempted to find out whether:

(i) Highly creative children differed significantly from their less creative peers in different areas of adjustments, such as home, health, social and school adjustment.

(ii) Highly creative children differed significantly from their less creative peers in adjustment to the problems stemming from the situation in which they found themselves, and

(iii) Whether better adjustment children differed from their maladjusted peers in creative performance.

The main findings were:

(i) None of the groups classified on the basis of creativity showed significant difference in health, social and school adjustment areas for the boys and girls.

(ii) The three creative groups among the boys showed significant difference in emotional adjustment.

(iii) Only two sub-groups (high and moderately-creative groups) of boys showed significant difference in home adjustment.

(iv) Although boys and girls differed significantly in adjustment to situations that are assumed to create problems for creative children the six sub-groups classified on the basis of creativity showed no significant differences.

(v) The better-adjusted and mal adjusted groups within each area of adjustment differed only in certain tasks of creativity and these tasks differed for each area of adjustment.

(vi) When classified on the basis of problems concerning personality characteristics of creative children the better adjusted and the maladjusted groups of boys differed in one task of creative (similarities) and the moderately adjusted and mal adjusted girls differed on one task (pattern meaning).

Pandey (1979) found that rural students secured better points in emotional, health and school adjustment areas. Urban students secured completely better marks in the aesthetic adjustment area. Significant relationship existed between adjustment, the level of aspiration and achievement. Urban students were facing difficulty in adjustment in school, health, and emotional areas.

Sharma (1979) conducted psychological study of adjustment problems of Harijans SC and backward class students of Agra district.

The enquiry was conducted:

(i) to study the adjustment of Harijans (HS), Scheduled Caste (SC) and Backward Class (BC) students who received financial help during 1975-77 and compare their adjustment position with that for the year 1964-65.

(ii) to know the comparative adjustment of HS, SC and BC, students belonging to different facilities and educational levels.

(iii) to study the adjustment of HS, SC and BC students of urban and rural settings.

(iv) to study the adjustment of HS, SC and BC students sex-wise and BC students of different socio-economic status.

The findings of the study were:

(i) The adjustment of HS, SC and BC students in 1965 was very unsatisfactory as against the conditions of GLC students, which was reported as satisfactory.

(ii) The adjustment of both the comparable group in 1977, indicate that the adjustment of HS, SC and BC group had considerably improved.

(iii) The faculty differences did not affect the adjustment scores and the levels of education were not related to the adjustment scores.

(iv) The urban students had higher adjustment scores on VPP than the rural students where as the urban students had higher maladjustment scores on ISB.

(v) The sex had significant effect on adjustment. The females had higher adjustment scores than the males and also the females had more psychological problems and complex than the males.

(vi) The socio-economic status had no effect on adjustment.

Mattoo (1980) in another study found generally adolescent at the lower intelligence level were the worst adjusted, and intelligent adolescents coming from poor homes had poor social and emotional adjustment. Boys were significantly superior to girls in emotional adjustment as to the girls of the same group. Girls of high intelligence were superior to high intelligent boys at the middle and low socio-economic status. The emotional adjustment of middle and low socio-economic status was inferior to that of their counterparts belonging to high socio-economic status. The two sexes also differed only in case of emotional but not social adjustment.

Reddy and Sudha (1980) conducted a study on adjustment of scheduled and non-scheduled caste students. The objective of the study was to compare the home, health, emotional and social adjustment of scheduled caste and non-scheduled caste students in relation to their educational and vocational aspiration and their socio-economic status.

The major findings of the study were (1) the educational aspiration has indicated significant difference in the total, home and health areas of adjustment where as the vocatioal aspiration has resulted in variation in the health area of adjustment only, (2) the low aspiration groups in both the cases were found to be maladjusted in home as regards to educational aspiration and in health as regards vocational aspiration, (3) the high aspiration group (educational) is found to be more maladjusted in total and also in health as compared to low aspiration group. But in the case of vocational aspiration, the low group is seen to be more maladjusted than the high vocational aspiration group of students, (4) there was no significant differences in the total adjustment of scheduled and non-scheduled students, but there was a significant difference in the social and emotional adjustment of these groups as it was found that the scheduled caste students had more problems of social adjustment and emotional adjustment than the non-scheduled caste students, (5) the residential students were more mal adjusted in all the four areas of adjustment as also in total than the non-residential students, (6) the girls were found to be more mal-adjusted than the boys in their social and emotional as also in total adjustment areas, (7) among the three groups of students belonging to low, middle and high socio-economic status, no significant difference was noticed in their home adjustment, health adjustment, social adjustment and total adjustment, (8) in the case of emotional adjustment it was found that the low and middle groups though did not differ between themselves, had more adjustment problems that the high group.

Saun (1980) reported the following conclusions:

(i) The male high and low achievers equally disclosed they are self to others in all the eight dimensions of SDI money, personality, study, body, interest, feelings-ideas, vocation and sex.

(ii) There was significant difference in self-disclosure in relation to five areas—money, body, interests, feelings, ideas and sex—among the female high and low achievers

(iii) There was significant difference in self-disclosure of the female high and low achievers towards their friends and teachers.

(iv) In the urban high and low achievers, there was significant difference in their mean self-disclosure scores so far as personality, body and sex were concerned.

(v) Towards friends, the urban high achievers disclosed more than their low achieving counterparts.

(vi) The rural low achievers disclosed themselves more significantly so far as sex was concerned. In the remaining seven areas both the groups had disclosed equally.

(vii) No significant difference was revealed in the level of self-disclosure of the rural high and low achievers.

(viii) The high school and intermediate level high achievers differed in their level of self-disclosure

in relation to money, study, interest and feeling ideas.

(ix) In the case of the male students towards brother, sister and friend, intermediate achievers disclosed more significantly than high school high achievers.

(x) The female high school and intermediate high achievers were equally connective in all the eight areas of self.

(xi) Significant difference existed between the high and low achieving female in health, social, emotional and educational areas of adjustment.

(xii) The male high achievers were more adjusted than the low achievers in the areas of home and health.

(xiii) The urban low achievers were emotionally more adjusted than the high achievers but they were equally adjusted in remaining areas of adjustment.

Singh (1981) studied adjusted problems of the SC and ST students in Residential schools of Rajasthan. The findings for the study were:

(i) Cumulative Record-cards of the students over a 3 year period indicated an improvement in performance among 26.6%, a consistent trend among 25.6%, decline in 28.9% cases and fluctuations in 5.9% students.

(ii) Regarding their socio-economic background, the majority belonged to agricultural class with parents in rural area, and the family size varying from five to eight members in large number of cases. Approximately 30% parents had a monthly income below the poverty line 64% of the family were literate.

(iii) Responses on the study habit revealed the presence of good study habits.

(iv) The majority suffered from fear, anxiety, and lack of self-confidence.

(v) Examinations and scholarship also caused worry and anxiety.

(vi) The majority had academic problems like poor handwriting, difficulties in English and Mathematics, lack of books and food.

(vii) They suffered from anxieties, uncertainty about future, unpleasant dreams, inferiority, indecision, particularly regarding vocations and higher education, retention of scholarship and the like.

(viii) By the large, they were free from heath problems. Interviews with heads, teachers, and wardens indicated that

(ix) Interviews with heads, teachers, and wardens indicated that the students were of average ability, having learning difficulties in English, Math and Physical Sciences while they performed well in games and sports.

(x) The teachers also felt that they suffered from an inferiority complex.

An attempt was made by Tripathi (1981) to study ljustment problems of undergraduates of Varanasi Division.

The following conclusions were drawn:

1. In all 40 per cent of the boys faced college environmental problems, 50 per cent faced economic problems, and 40 per cent could not develop amicable relation with their classmates.
2. The problems of 53 per cent of girls concerned spending leisure time, 47 per cent were about lack of educational environment in the college.

3. About 53 per cent of the urban and 42 per cent of the rural students faced difficulties in their adjustment with the educational environment.
4. Girls were comparatively more adjusted to the home area. Highly adjusted students secured better points on the intelligence test. Urban boys and girls were superior, in this respect to residents of rural areas.
5. Adjusted students had comparatively better socio-economic background.
6. Girls secured better points on the socio-economic status scale.
7. Intelligence and adjustment were mutually dependent.
8. Maladjusted students faced difficulty in maintaining domestic adjustment, economic crisis, educational environment, leisure time activities, etc. However girls faced less difficulty in adjusting to these situations.

The findings of the study of Sultana (1983) were:

1. The adolescents showed a trend towards internal locus of control (ILC)
2. They had low purpose in life (LPIL)
3. Girls were better adjusted than boys with regard to home were.
4. High purpose in life group students were better adjusted to their home than those having LPIL and other levels of PIL.
5. Adolescents with different PIL orientations differed in their health adjustment, adjustment to society, emotional adjustment, and educational adjustment and overall adjustment.
6. The girls were educationally better adjusted than boys.

7. Compared to 'externals', 'internals' adolescents were emotionally better adjusted.

8. The girls were, on the whole better adjusted than boys.

9. The interaction effect of sex and PIL was significant.

Lata (1985) studied the impact of parental attitude on social, emotional and educational adjustment of normal and handicapped children. It was found that normal children differed significantly from handicapped children in adjustment. Normal boys and handicapped girls showed better emotional adjustment than normal girls and handicapped boys. Normal students did not differ significantly from the handicapped in the field of social adjustment. Normal students differed significantly from the handicapped students in the field of educational adjustment. Parental attitude did not significantly affect the adjustment of normal students. The attitude of parents affected significantly the adjustment of handicapped girls but did not affect the adjustment of handicapped boys.

Banel (1986) found that:

The best adjustment of foreigners was in the academic area and the worst in the physical area. Over all adjustment of NV (Fiji) was the best and that of Uganda and Zaire the worst. The typical problems of adjustment which were experienced by more than 60% of the foreign students were lack of accommodation, inadequate medical care, non-availability of telephone facility, lack of clean water and water-cooler, unappetizing food and home-sickness. The academic performance of the students was average. A sizable section of foreign students did not find the methods of teaching in Indian Universities up to their expectation.

Saraswat (1986) conducted a study on adjustment of adolescents. Basically it was aimed at finding out the levels of various adjustments of boys and girls. A sample of 840 students was drawn from 14 schools of Government Higher Secondary Schools under Delhi Administration. Saxena's

(1962) Adjustment Scale (Hindi) was used to measure the adjustment of boys and girls. It was reported that boys and girls differed significantly on health adjustment, social adjustment, and school adjustment and on the total adjustment. On all these four adjustment areas girls were found to be better adjusted as compared to boys.

The study of Sharma (1986) revealed that non-professional college students faced more adjustment problems than professional college students in the area of home adjustment. Arts students had greater adjustment problems in home and health areas than engineering students, where as engineering students had greater adjustment problems in social areas than arts students. Arts and teacher training students had no significant differences in adjustment problems. Science students had greater adjustment problems than medical student in home areas. Science students had greater adjustment problems than Law students in health, social, emotional and educational areas. Medical students had more adjustment problems than commerce students in social, emotional and educational areas. Teacher Training College students had greater adjustment problems than Commerce students in home, health and emotional areas while Commerce students had poor adjustment than teacher training students in educational area.

The study of Sunita (1986) indicated the following findings:

1. The scores of sample subjects on motor ability for the whole were not distributed normally. The mean score for motor ability for boys was 143.05, and for girls it was 132.50, with SD of 29.39 and 30.60 respectively.

2. Boys who performed better in motor ability also had better home adjustment.

3. Girls were better adjusted at home than boys.

4. Boys scored more on motor ability than girls.

5. Motor ability played a positive role in promoting social adjustment.

6. Boys were more socially adjusted than girls.
7. The co-efficient of correlation between social adjustment and motor ability was more in boys than girls.
8. Motor ability and emotional adjustment were positively related.
9. Boys were more emotionally adjusted than girls.
10. The coefficient of correlation between motor ability and emotional adjustment was higher in boys than in girls.

Singh and Singh (1987) conducted a study on adjustment behaviour on adolescents in relation to caste and surroundings.

For the purpose a sample of 180 pupils belonging to higher backward and Scheduled Caste students from rural and urban settings of Sultanpur District of U.P. were chosen. The data were collected using the Adjustment Inventory of Sinha and Singh (1993).

The findings of the study were:

(i) the pupils of both the groups i.e. higher caste and backward caste differed from each other significantly with respect to their social adjustment patterns and the difference was in favour of the students of higher caste, (ii) as regards educational adjustment and emotional adjustment both the aforesaid groups did not differ significantly from each other, (iii) however pupils belonging to higher caste were found to be emotionally, socially and educationally more mature than their counterparts, (iv) pupils of rural areas differed significantly from their urban counterparts in respect to emotional and educational adjustment i.e. rural pupils appear to be less adjusted than their urban counterparts on emotional and educational adjustment, (v) rural pupils scored high on social adjustment pattern than the urban pupils, but the surroundings does not have an affect on the social adjustment behaviour of pupils. (vi) both these groups of pupils showing very unsatisfactory adjustment belonged to urban area which may be due to their poor surroundings and educational facilites.

A combined qualitative and quantitative research design was used by Cheng (1989) to examine the initial adjustment of Chinese and Korean graduate students to a large university in the United States. The instruments of this research included an interview guide, the Adjective Checklist, the State Trait Anxiety Inventory, the Rotter's I.E. Locus of Control Scale and the Semantic Differential Sixteen Chinese students and six Korean students volunteered to participate in this study over a seven month time period.

The findings of this quantitative research indicated that the entire group of subjects evaluated "Me, As I would like to Be" lower the longer they stayed in the United States. The Chinese subjects and Korean subjects evaluated "The Past" differently on four out of six occasions that this instrument was administered. The male subjects evaluated "my Home Country" higher than the female subjects. The Chinese subjects evaluated 'my Home Country" and "Me, As I Actually Am", higher than the Korean subjects. The Korean subjects had higher trait anxiety than the Chinese subjects.

The result obtained from the Adjective Checklist showed that the majority of the subjects had positive self-image. They were concerned about how they related interpersonally and attempted to avoid having conflict with people.

The interview data suggested that the four primary factors affecting the adjustment of the Chinese and Korean graduates to the United States were their personal characteristics, their English abilities, their academic performance, and the social support they felt from significant others. The subjects gradually became less anxious about their academic performance and more anxious about their interpersonal relationships as they stayed in the United States.

The study of Mckay (1990) compared the psychological competence and level of adjustment to college of learning disabled and non-handicapped community college students. The relationship among psychological competence, adjustment to college, and academic success was also examined.

The sample consisted of 44 learning disabled and 44 non-handicapped students identified by five random selected colleges within the North Carolina Community College system. The subjects were contracted by a staff member of their respective colleges and asked to complete a four-part questionnaire. In addition to demographic question, the questionnaire included measures of social competence, affective competence (emotionally stability, shyness and self-assurance), and level of academic, social and affective adjustment to college.

The results of a one-way ANOVA indicate non-significant difference between learning disabled and non-handicapped students for the variables social and affective competence (including emotional stability, shyness, and self-assurance). Significant difference were found between the two groups for the variables overall, academic, social and affective adjustment to college. Social competence, emotional stability and self-assurance were significantly related to adjustment to college for the total sample. None of these variables were significant for the subgroup of non-handicapped students. Social competence was significantly related to the level of adjustment of college for learning disabled students.

Although the regression models were not significant, due to limited variation and degrees of freedom, psychosocial competence and the measures of college adjustment were able to explain 34.6% of the variation in grade point averages of the non-handicapped students and 20.0% of the variation for the learning disables students. A discriminate analysis model based on measures of psychosocial competence and college adjustment correctly classified 72.7% of the learning disabled and non-handicapped students.

Agarwal and Sonawat (1991) compared home, health, social, emotional, education and overall adjustment of college students, belonging to Arts, Science and Commerce disciplines. They concluded that both Arts and Commerce students were found to possess home adjustment to the same degree. Also, their study indicated that home adjustment means scores of Arts and Science groups differ significantly from each other. Further, the study showed that the three groups, namely, Arts, Science and Commerce, differ significantly from each other with respect to health adjustment. Again, the students of Arts, Science and Commerce were found to possess social adjustment to the same extent, and Arts students were found to be superior to other two groups in emotional adjustment.

Sharma and Mehta (1993) conducted a study to see the effect of psychological discordance between chosen curriculum viz. Science and scientific interest upon psychological adjustment and academic achievement.

Tools used to collect data included Chatterji's CNPR-962 (interest scale), Adjustment Inventory for school students by A.K.P. Sinha and R.P. Singh and the percentage of marks obtained by the subjects in Class X annual examination. The collected data were treated by Mean and ANOVA.

The findings of the study were:

(1) Subjects having psychological discordance between choosen curriculum were found to have significantly lower psychological adjustment in comparison to subjects having concordance. There was a significant effect not only on the total adjustment but also on the individual areas of emotional and educational adjustment. This type of discordance did not affect social adjustment. (2) Subjects having psychological discordance between chosen curriculums were found to have significantly lower academic achievement in comparison to subjects having concordance (0207).

Kukreti (1994) found that the preadolescent boys belonging to SVM Saraswati Vidya Mandir, GJHS (i.e., Govt. Junior High School) had scored sufficiently higher mean value on social adjustment than CS (Convent School) boys. While in comparison to SVM boys the CS boys were found emotionally better adjusted. The boys of SVM and CS had possessed better emotional adjustment than the boys of GJHS. In all areas of adjustment (emotional, social and educational as well as total) the pre-adolescent girls studying in SVM were found to have higher mean score than the girls of CS. In comparison to GJHS girls the girls of SVM showed significantly better educational and total adjustment. When all preadolescent boys and girls of each school were considered together in respect of total adjustment, the students of SVM were found having better adjustment than CS and GJHS students. On social adjustment variable, the students of SVM and GJHS had secured comparatively higher mean values than CS students. On educational adjustment, SVM and CS students were found to have significantly higher mean scores than the students of GJHS.

Kumar, Prasad and Prasad (1995) studied adjustment patterns of physically handicaps. The objective was to study the impact of physical handicaps on adjustment of respondents. Mohsin-Shamshad-Khurshid-Jehan-Adjustment Inventory was used to collect the data for the study. The collected data were treated with Mean, SD and *'t'* ratio. It was found that the normal and the handicapped subjects differed significantly in their home adjustment, social adjustment, and emotional adjustment as well as in overall adjustment. The normal and the handicapped subject did not differ significantly only on health adjustment.

Kumar, Singh, and Mohammad (1995) found that different dimensions of adjustment were not found to be significant. Caste had significant effect on adjustment. Community had no significant effect on the adjustment of adolescents. The science and arts group students differed significantly on all dimensions of adjustment in favour of science group.

Aminabhavi (1996) conducted a study on adjustment ability of physically disabled and abled students and found that:

(1) Physically disabled students scored more than abled students in all the variables, which indicated that they

were maladjusted with family, emotion, mood and leadership aspects, and average in their adjustment with social reality and criminality aspect. (2) Physically disabled and abled students differed significantly in their adjustment with emotion, mood, criminality and leadership, while they didn't differ significantly in their remaining areas. (3) Physically disables students were significantly low in their adjustment with emotion, mood, criminality and leadership, as compared to physically abled students.

Sharma and Gakhar (1994) compared the adjustment of students of denominational schools.

The objectives of the study were to find out and compare the home, health, social, and overall adjustment of students of different denominational schools. Adjustment Inventory (Mittal, 1976) was the tool used. Based on the results of *'t'* test for adjustment following findings were drawn:

1. Home adjustment of students of Sanatan Dharam Schools is better than those in other denominational schools. This is followed by students of DAV/Arya Samaj, which is further followed by students of Khalsa/Singh Sabha Schools.

2. Students of Khals/Singh Sabha Schools are well adjusted on health adjustment, followed by students of Convent and of DAV/Arya Samaj Schools.

3. On social adjustment, students of DAV/Arya Samaj are well adjusted, followed by students of Convent and Sanatan Dharam Schools.

4. In social adjustment, students of Convent Schools are well adjusted, as compared to other students.

5. Over-all adjustment of students of DAV/Arya Samaj Schools is high followed by students of Sanatan Dharam and Khals/Singh Sabha School.

Kasinath (2000) studied student's adjustment and its relation to organizational climate in Jawahar Navodaya Vidyalayas.

Two objectives of the study were:

(i) to compare the emotional, social, educational and total adjustment of boys and girls studying in JNVs and

(ii) to compare the emotional, social, educational and total adjustments of urban and rural students studying in JNVs.

The findings of the study were as follows:

1. The boys and girls studying in JNVs differ significantly in their emotional adjustment. As the mean of the emotional adjustment of boys is greater than that of girls, it may be concluded that boys were more emotionally unstable in JNVs than girls.

2. The boys and girls in JNVs do not differ significantly in their social and educational adjustments.

3. The boys and girls in JNVs differ significantly in their total adjustment. Further, higher mean of total adjustment score for boys indicated that general adjustment score of boys in JNVs is lower than that of girls.

4. The urban and rural students studying in JNVs do not differ significantly in their emotional, social, educational and total adjustment.

2. Adjustment and Achievement

The relationship between adjustment and achievement has been the subject of study for many scholars in India and in other countries.

George (1966) concluded that:

1. The pupils with high intelligence were identified as better-adjusted and high achievers in all the groups studied.

2. Extraversion was related to only a few areas in adjustment and had no influence on achievement.

3. The less neurotic were better adjusted in all areas.

4. Neuroticism had significant influence on achievement.

5. Interaction effect of intelligence and streams on adjustment scores was significant in school and health adjustment.

Guta (1981) found that:

(i) adolescents from joint families tended to exhibit significantly better educational, social and health adjustment, emotional adjustment and home adjustment were independent of family type. A higher desirability of parental preferences in the social field resulted in better educational adjustment, (ii) though achievement was a function of socio-economic status, it was independent of family size and type; (iii) an inverse relationship existed between the desirability of parental preferences and the achievement of adolescents; (iv) low desirability of parental preferences resulted in significantly higher delinquency among average achievers. Those with low level of achievement and adjustment were significantly more delinquent; (v) creativity was manifest significantly more among those with poor and average achievement; (vi) students with poor achievement were more creative when desirability of parental preferences was of average level. Students with high and average adjustment were significantly more creative.

Swain and Panda (1982) conducted a study on adjustment differences among adolescent boys and girls at different levels of academic achievement.

The objectives of the study were:

1. to investigate whether there exists a significant difference in adjustment among adolescent boys and girls, 2. to find the difference in adjustment of boys and girls at high, middle and low level of academic

achievement. To study the personal, social and total adjustment of adolescent Reddy's (1964) "Adolescent Adjustment Inventory" was used and to the academic achievement students aggregate marks at the H.S.C Examination (Class XI) were taken from their records.

To analyse and interpret the test scores, the statistical procedure of one way 'analysis of variance' was adopted and when the value of F-ratio became significant, Tukey test was followed.

The major findings of the study were:

1. there was no significant difference among high, middle and low achievers boys, in relation to their personal adjustment, 2. there was no significant difference among high, middle and low achiever boys in relation to their social adjustment, 3. there were significant differences in total adjustment of boys. High achiever boys were well adjusted than the boys at middle and low levels of academic achievement and the boys of middle academic achievement have equal chances of adjustment with the boys of low academic achievement, 4. there was no significant difference among high, middle and low achiever girls in relation to their personal adjustment, 5. there was no significant difference among, high, middle and low achievers girls in relation to their social adjustment, 6. there were significant differences in the total adjustment of girls i.e. high and middle achievere girls and more adjusted than the low achiever girls and also there were equal chance of adjustment between high and middle achiever girls.

Kapoor (1987) found that high achievers had better home, health, social, emotional and school adjustment. The overall adjustment scores of high achievers were also significantly higher than the overall adjustment scores of the other two groups.

The study of Estridge (1989) investigated the relationship between adjustment and levels of English class placement among tenth grade public high school students. The California Test of Personality was utilized to obtain measures of personal, social and total adjustment for the 457 students tested in this study.

All students were placed in enriched, academic, or general levels of tenth grade English classes. Subjects included the entire tenth grade population of a public high school of approximately 1600 students in a small southern city. Students placed in Special Education Resource classes or unusual levels of class placement for which they would not ordinarily qualify were tested, but their test results were omitted from the study.

Three hypotheses were formulated for investigation. An analysis of variance was performed on the data to determine whether significant relationship between variables of adjustment and level of class placement existed. The statistical technique of testing was performed to determine whether academic achievement acting as a variable within a group for variables (academic, level of class placement, sex and race) influence scores on individual adjustment categories. The required level of significance was 0.05.

Results of the analysis of variance testes indicated that there is a significance of difference in total adjustment, with students in higher levels of English class placement scoring higher and those in lower levels of scoring lower in the adjustment measure. However, means scores for levels showed that none of the groups scored at or above the 50th percentile, which is the level necessary for satisfactory or superior adjustment by the test manual definitions. Academic achievement did not appear to the significantly related to scores on any category of adjustment. Therefore hypotheses 2 and 3 rejected.

Zarghouni (1989) conducted a study to examine the perceptions of international students attending a predominantly black urban university and a predominantly white urban university towards the adjustment problems that the experience in their universities. Also, the study was designed to determine the significant differences between the academic success of international students attending a predominantly black urban university and of those attending a pre dominantly white urban university.

The population consisted of 3,079 internationals students enrolled at Texas Southern University and the University of Houston during the summer session of 1986. A sample size of 621 students was randomly selected from the population of international students. From the problems stated, eight null hypotheses were stated and tested.

To analyze the data, the researcher utilized the *t*-test to determine whether there was a significant difference between the means academic success (GPA) of international students attending a predominantly black urban university and those attending a predominantly white urban university. The. 05 level of significance was pre-established as a criterion of statistical significance. The finding: of this study were there was no significant difference between the academic success of international students attending Texas Southern University and of those attending the University of Houston as affected by sex or age. However, there was a significant difference between the academic success of graduate subjects attending Texas Southern and of those attending the University of Houston with regard to their academic status.

Using a longitudinal design Chartrand (1990) examined the academic and personal adjustment of students who simultaneously held one or more of the following roles employee, parent, or partner Participants completed an initial questionnaire (N = 425) at the beginning of fall quarter 1987 and a follow-up questionnaire (N = 284) at the beginning of spring quarter 1988. Role commitment, role strain, role gratification, self-role congruence, personal adjustment, and academic adjustment were operationalised to investigate the effect of combining the student role with other roles-questionnaire data were used to address four different research agendas: (a) gender comparions of role perceptions and experiences, (b) estimation of perceived similarity of a god student, a good employee, a good parents and a good partner along dimensions of evaluation, power and activity, (c) prediction of specific role conflicts and role gratification, and (d) causal modeling of interrelationships between students role evaluation, student role commitment, self-good student role congruence, personal adjustment and academic adjustment. Conclusions were directed towards multiple role theory and potential interventions that promote the development multiple role students.

Fox (1990) studied the effects of relocation and family structure upon academic achievement and behavioural adjustment of 14 eight-grade students.

An intensive case study design with multiple cases was used to study post-relocation academic achievements and behavioural adjustment of 14 eighth grade students. Students, parents, and two teachers for each student were interviewed in a new school. Interview data were analyzed to determine in the effects of relocation within different family structures. Additional variable were examined to determine their role in mediating post-relocation effects. These variables were attitude towards relocation, class size, extended support systems, number of previous relocation, pre-relocation behaviour, sense of perfōrmance of this move, socio-economic status and teacher expectations for post-relocation behaivour and academic achievement. He found no change in academic achievement could be identified when mediating variable were not considered. However, those students who were first born and the who lived with two biological or step a parents displayed higher post-relocation academic achievement than did their counterparts from other family structures. Improvements were noted in post-relocation behavioural adjustment. Those students, who lived with two biological or step-parents, demonstrated the greatest improvement. Birth order did not appear to mediate the effects of relocation on subsequent behaivoural adjustment.

Beaty (1991) attempted to determine whether or not there is a relationship between these students self-esteem and social provisions and their level of academic achievement. Also, it sought to ascertain if there are substantial differences between visually handicapped and non-handicapped students on these variables.

Results indicated that there were no significant differences between groups on self-esteem or social provisions, however, visually handicapped students significantly out-scored non-handicapped students on college grade—point average. There was no evidence of a significant prediction of grade point average by the non-intellective variables for either group, controlling for mean high school grades. Tests of correlation did reveal that self-esteem and social provisions functioned differently for blind low vision and sighted students.

Rongali (1993) studied adjustment in relation to social integration and achievement of the students of residential schools. The major findings were:

(1) there was no significant relationship between adjustment and social integration, (2) adjustment achievement and social integration were significantly related, (3) there was a significant and negative relationship between adjustment and social integration of students of AP Residential Schools, (4) there was a significant and positive relationship between adjustment and achievement of students of AP Residential Schools, APSW Residential Schools, AP Residential Schools for general and AP Residential Schools for boys, (5) there was a significant and positive relationship between social integration and achievement of students of AP Residential Schools and APSW Residential Schools, (6) there was a significant and negative relationship between social integration and achievement of students of AP Residential Schools for general and AP Residential Schools for girls, (7) in terms of adjustments, achievement and social integration, there were significant differences between AP Residential Schools and APSW Residential Schools, (8) boys and girls differed significantly on adjustment, social integration and achievement, (9) there were significant differences among Scheduled Caste, Scheduled Tribe and other castes in respect of adjustment, social integration and achievement.

Sethy (1993) conducted a study on adjustment differences among adolescent boys and girls at different levels of academic achievement.

The objectives of the study were.

(1) to find out the difference in adjustment of boys and girls at high, middle and low levels of academic achievement, (2) to investigate whether there exists a significant difference in adjustment between adolescent boys and girls.

The findings of the study were:

1. High, middle and low achievers were found to differ significantly in relation to their personal adjustment. The mean adjustment sense indicates that high achieving boys were having better personal adjustment than the low achieving boys.

2. There are significant differences in the total adjustment of boys. The result of 't' test indicates that high achieving boys are better adjusted than the low achieving boys.

3. High, middle and low achieving girls were found to differ significantly in their personal, social and total adjustment. The 't' results indicate that high and lower achieving girls differed significantly in their total adjustment. But in personal adjustment there were significant differences between high achieving girls and low achieving girls and between middle achiever and low achiever girls. But high and middle girls achiever did not differ in their personal adjustment. In social adjustment there was significant difference between high and low achieving girls and high achieving girls were found to be better adjustment than the low achieving girls.

Chouhan and Murthy (1994) studied the effect of achievement on adjustment of deprived adolescents. The objectives of the study were to examine the effect of scholastic achievement on adjustment of adolescents of Scheduled Castes, Scheduled Tribes and General Caste groups.

It was found that (1) subjects belonging to general caste were better adjusted as compared to subjects of Scheduled Castes and Tribes of which Scheduled Tribes students were found to least adjusted, (2) male adolescents were found better adjusted as compared to female adolescents, (3) high soholastic achievers were better adjusted as compared to low scholastic achievers, (4) there was a significant difference in the adjustment of high achievers and low achievers, (5) both, caste as well as sex did not yield significant main effect on the adjustment of the deprived adolescents, (6) adjustment of deprived adolescents was found to be significantly affected by their scholastic achievement. High achievers showed better adjustment whereas low achievers displayed poor adjustment, (7) male adolescents were found better adjusted than females, (8) adolescents belonging to general caste were found to be better adjusted than Scheduled Castes and Scheduled Tribes.

Kaile and Kaur (1995) undertook a study on adjustment of over and under achievers in mother tongue. The objectives of the study were: (i) to find out the relationship between adjustment (social, emotional and educational) and achievement in mother tongue, and (ii) to find out whether over and under achievers in mother tongue differ significantly in their adjustment. Group Test of General Mental Ability of Jalota and Singh (Punjabi Version) and Adjustment Inventory for school students of Sinha and Singh were administered on students to collect data for the study. The statistical techniques used to analyse data were Pearson's product Moment Correlation, Regression Analysis and Critical Ratio.

It was found that social adjustment did not have significant relationship with achievement in mother tongue while emotional adjustment and educational adjustment did. No significant difference existed in adjustment (social, emotional and educational) of over and under achievers.

Nair (1999) conducted a study on certain personality and familial variables discriminating between over and under achievers in Secondary School Science and Mathematics. The sample of the study consisted of 1758 pupils studying in standard IX of the schools in the state of Kerala.

Proportionate stratified sampling giving representation to sex, local and type of management were used for the selection of the sample.

The study revealed that (i) there was no significant difference in social adjustment between the under-achievers and over achievers in Science, (ii) as regards the personal adjustment no significant difference was also noted between the two groups in personal adjustment, (iii) on the other hand the under achievers and over achievers in Mathematics differed significantly in their social adjustment and personal adjustment and the differences were in favour of the over achievers in mathematics.

3. Adjustment and other Variables

A number of investigators have conducted studies on adjustment in relation to some variables. They are presented below:

Goswami (1980) found that: (1) the number of problems increased with age, (ii) the adolescent girls encountered maximum number of problems in the emotional and mental areas followed by the problems in the school and study and home areas. The physical and sexual was the leas problem encountering area, (iii) class-wise analysis of the problems revealed that the girls of class VIII encountered maximum number of problems in the areas of home and school and study followed by emotional and mental areas. The social, religious, moral, physical and sexual areas took the fourth and fifth positions respectively, (iv) in class IX and X the emotional, mental, school and study were the most problematic areas followed by home, social, religious, moral, physical and sexual areas.

Mattoo (1980) undertook a study on social and emotional adjustment patterns of adolescents boys and girls at various levels of socio-economic status and general intelligence.

One of the objectives of the study was to test the significance of the differences in social and emotional adjustment of adolescent boys and girls of different levels (higher, middle and lower) of general intelligence and socio-economic status.

The findings with regards to effect of socio-economic status were as follows:

The differences in the adjustment of adolescents of the three levels of socio-economic strata have been found significant in the emotional adjustment only. The difference in social adjustment was not significant because in our society the adolescents move within the social circle of their socio-stratum.

The emotional adjustment of adolescents of the middle and the lower strata of society though almost at par, was significantly inferior to that of their counterparts of the higher stratum. This was probably due to the financial stringency at home, which creates a lot of problems and worries. The two sexes differ from one another in the emotional adjustment only.

Srivastava (1980) concluded that, there was substantial correlation between intelligence and achievement and moderate correlation between achievement and socio-economic status and between intelligence and socio-economic status. Scientific, clerical interest and educational adjustment were substantially correlated with achievement. Mechanical interest and emotional and social adjustment also had significant positive correlation with achievement.

Kamalesh (1981) made an attempt to make a comparative study of self-concept, adjustment, interests, and motivating among the SC and non-SC students.

The main findings of the study were: (1) Non-SC students from the urban area belonging to higher socio-economic status had brighter self-concept than the SC students belonging to lower socio-economic status, (2) The level of adjustment among the urban SC students belonging to lower socio-economic status was below normal, (3) The non ST students, both in the urban and the rural areas did not have adjustment problems.

Kumari (1982) reported the following findings.

1. The difference in achievement of various socio-metric groups was significant.

2. Populars accounted for significant differences from other socio-metric groups, i.e. neglects, isolates and rejects, on the variable of achievement. Popular showed the highest mean score on achievement followed by the mean scores of isolates, rejectee and neglectees.

3. The different socio-metric groups differed significantly on the variables on home adjustment, social adjustment, health and emotional adjustment, school adjustment and total adjustment.

4. Populars got the highest mean score on home adjustment.

5. On the variable of social adjustment the group combination of populars and neglectees, popular and isolates, popular, and rejectees and neglectees and rejectees attained significant differences between their means.

6. In school adjustment the popular were the best. They had the highest mean score (55.04) followed by isolates, neglectees and rejectees.

7. In total adjustment, populars had the highest mean score (221.68) 10 F-ratio was significant for the variable of socio-economic status indicating the existence of differences among various socio metric groups.

8. In the case of neglectees all the correlation values were positive between different variables of adjustments.

9. There was a positive relationship between intelligence and home adjustment for all the socio-metric groups.

10. There was a positive correlation between achievement and total adjustment for populars, neglectees, isolates, and rejectees.

11. The product-moment coefficient of correlation in respect of socio-metric categories ranged from 0.146 to 0.439 for variables of total adjustment and socio-economic status.

Saraswat (1982) conducted a study on self-concept in relation to adjustment, values, academic achievement, socio-economic status and sex of high school students of Delhi and found that: the boys' self-concept was positively and significantly related to social adjustment, while the girls' self-concept was positively and significantly related to home, health, social, emotional, school as well as total adjustment. The boys' self-concept was positively significantly related to political and religious values, while the girls' self-concept was not related to any of these values. Only intellectual self-concept was positively and significantly related to academic achievement in both the sexes. Boys and girls differed significantly on total self-concept and its physical, social and moral dimensions. Girls were found to be higher on all these dimensions.

Annamma (1984) concluded that a majority of the college students were conformists, with a stable system of values, and without rebellious tendencies. The younger college students were more spiritualism oriented as compared to the older group which was more materialism oriented. Female students were seen to be better adjusted than male students in all the areas studied.

The study of Kumar (1985) revealed that (i) the gifted children were better adjusted in health and least adjusted in school as compared with other areas of adjustment; (ii) the gifted and the average children did not differ in their total adjustment; (ii) the gifted boys had better total adjustment than the gift girls. They were more adjusted in health, emotional and school areas than the gifted girls. But there was no difference in their home and social adjustment;

(iv) the average boys had better total adjustment than the average girls. But there was no difference in their home and health adjustment; (v) there was no difference in the total problems of the gifted and average children; (vi) the gifted girls and average girls had more emotional problems than the gifted boys. But there was difference in their home, health, social and school problems; (vii) the analysis of the problem checklist indicated that there was no difference in the nature of the problems faced by the gifted and the average; (viii) the gifted and the average did not differ in their satisfaction of basic needs but differed in the satisfaction of higher order needs; (ix) among esteem and educational needs, the gifted were less satisfied in their need for achievement, intellectual curiosity, research and problem solving and encouragement of creative thinking than the average. However, there was no difference in their satisfaction of needs for intellectual independent study habits.

Sharma (1985) reported that the emotional, educational, and total adjustment of students determined their academic sub-culture. Health, social and emotional dimensions of adjustment were significantly correlated with collegiate sub-culture.

The study of Anshu (1988) showed that family climate was an effective determinant of home adjustment of the adolescent. Regarding school adjustment of adolescents family climate was found to be effective but its influence was found to be more prominent in the case of urban adolescents. Family climate was found to be significantly responsible for the emotional adjustment of adolescents irrespective of their locality and sex.

Mary (1989) found that what occurred in the Behaviour and Adjustment class—the active engagement in learning, a variety of control techniques. The ongoing evaluation and modification by the teacher was associated with the class room teacher's and/or student's perspective. The classroom teacher's perspective was shaped by his goals and beliefs about education as well as his interactions. The students' perspective was shaped by symbolic interaction.

The contributions of family-level cognitive, and achievement variables to the behaviour problems and social competency of children (N = 114), ages 5-14, grades K-8, referred for learning disability evaluations was explored by Mittelmeier (1989) using standardized assessment instruments. Participants were selected from a child development clinic in a large urban teaching hospital. Measures included: Family information form, Hollingshead Four-factor Index of Social status, vide Range Achievement Test (WRAT), Peabody Individual Achievement Test (PIAT), University of Rhode Island. Finally Functioning Scale (URIEFS), Family Adaptability and Cohension Evaluation Scale (FACES II), and the Child Behaviour Checklist (CBCL), Behaviour Problems and Social Competency Scales). Multivariate statistical analyses (including multivariate analyses of variance, discriminate function and classification analyses) suggested that the family rituals, contributed significantly to children's adjustment both for behaviour problems and social competency, sensitivity (correct classification of Higher Behaviour problem group) and specificity (correct classification of the Low Behaviour problem group) of family functioning, cognitive and achievement variables was approximately 71% for both groups. Family Rituals, Family conflict, IQ and Achievement emerged as important predictors of children's behaviour problems. For social competency, results of the discriminate function and follow up classification analysis indicated that specificity was superior to sensitivity with these values being equal to 69% and 75% respectively. Family communication, Achievement, Family conflict, Family Rituals and family worrier contributed to the correct classification of children's group membership on the basis of social competency. For both behaviour problems and social competency, certain types of family patterns emerged.

The study of Razavi (1989) assessed self-perceived problems of international students in three community colleges in the Washington D.C. Metropolitan areas. The study also sought to determine whether sex, national origin, marital status and length of stay in the United States were significant factors influencing the type of and number of adjustment problems. The Michigan International student problem Inventory was employed to collect data for the study; 1,556 students were surveyed.

Length of stay in he United States was found to have a positive influence in resolving problems pertaining to admission-selection, orientation, placement and language. Male students generally experienced more problems than older students (e.g., freshmen reported more problems than sophomores). No significant differences were found concerning the number of problems experienced by international students in the three selected community colleges. The most serious problems experienced by international students included orientation, admissions, academic, social and financial needs all of which are more or less under the direct influence of the college themselves.

Adolescents with cystic fibrosis were studied by Guidry (1990) in order to investigate personal and environmental resources, which influence individual differences in adaptation level. Specially, it was hypothesized that relationship with parents and peers would serve to increase the relationship between problem-solving skills and adjustment such that well-developed skills and satisfactory relationship would facilitate the development of adaptive behaviour. Adjustment was defined in terms of maximal physical functioning and age-appropriate psychosocial behaviour. Against prediction, a canonical correlation procedure revealed no significant dimensions along which the set of adjustment variables and the set of copying variables were related. Reasons for this lack of findings were discussed, and regression analysis was than performed on each adjustment variable separately. The prediction of physical functioning yielded non-significant results, which was also contrary to expectations. Results indicated that, after controlling forage, subject's interpersonal problem-solving skills failed to predict their level of psychosocial adjustment. However, it was found that parent's autonomous (well-differentiate) reactions to their adolescents and subject's supportive relationship with a significant peer were the strongest contributors to differences in psychosocial functioning.

Haynes (1990) reported that (a) psychological adjustment was related to positive attitudes towards cooperation in male and female students and female non-students, (b) positive attitudes towards cooperation were related to dyadic adjustment in female non-students, but not in the other groups, (c) positive attitudes towards competition were not related to psychological or dyadic adjustment, (d) positive attitudes towards individualism were negatively related to psychological adjustment in all four groups, and (e) positive attitudes towards individualism were found to be negatively related to dyadic adjustment in male and female students and in female non-students.

The study of Lou (1990) sought to identify the adjustment problems of Chinese students in U.S. to find out how they resolve the problems, and to analyze the relationship between adjustment problems and their demographic variables, including age, sex areas of study, marital status, location of spouse, sources of financial support, and length of stay in the U.S. Questionnaires were mailed to 500 Chinese students in ten Universities, 268 were returned. Interviews of twenty Chinese students were conducted. The data were analyzed by means of a variety of statistical procedures which include examinations of descriptive statistics and analysis of variance.

The findings of the study were: (1) significant relationship existed between the ages of Chinese students and their adjustment problems. (2) Significant relationship existed between the marital status of Chinese students and their adjustment problems. (3) The tests of sub-hypotheses indicated that (a) the age of Chinese students was relevant to English and Communication problems, (b) the areas of study were relevant to English and communication problems, (c) the marital status was relevant to health problems, (d) the sources of financial support were relevant to financial problems, and (e) the length of stay was relevant to English and communication problems. (4) Overall, the major adjustment problems of Chinese students are English and Communication problems, social and cultural problems and financial problems. (5) Most Chinese students resolved their problems by practicing, persisting in theirs effort, learning by doing and seeking help from others. (6) Finally, an overwhelming majority of Chinese students believe that their educational experiences in the U.S. are worthwhile and rewarding.

Chaurasia (1993) made an attempt to study creativity in relation to adjustment and aggression. The tool used to collect data included Creativity Test of Passi; Adjustment Inventory of Srivastava and Srivastava and Aggression Questionnaire of Pati. The collected data were treated with mean, S.D. and 't' values. The findings to the study were: (1) When different levels of adjustment were compared for their creativity performance, they were found to differ significantly. (2) When different levels of aggression were compared for their creativity performance, they were found to differ significantly.

Keshap (1933) concluded that the boys and girls differed significantly on adjustment. The adjustment and narcism motive were found to be positively and significantly related.

Rajamankkam and Vasanthal (1933) studied the adjustment problems of adolescent students in relation to their achievements. The objectives of the study were: (i) to find out whether there is any relationship between students adjustment problems and level of school achievements, (ii) to know whether the influence of adjustment on achievement of students, and (iii) to find out whether the number of siblings, parents', qualification, occupational status of the parents have any influence upon students adjustment problems and achievements.

It was found that (1) there was a significant positive correlation between adjustment and achievement. It was found that as the number of siblings decreased the adjustment scores increased but the achievement scores increased and vice-versa was true, (2) the different sibling groups differed significantly on achievement, (3) it was found that the scores of the students on their adjustment gradually decreased as the qualification of the parents increased while on achievement score gradually increased as the qualification of parents increased, (4) as regards parental occupational status, it was found that children of those parents on different occupation did not differ among themselves on their adjustment and their achievement.

Manju (1994) studied adjustment as a function of sense of humour degree of aggression and inferiority feeling and found that (1) there was a significant effect of sense of humour on the total adjustment, (2) inferiority feelings highly effected total adjustment, (3) there was no interaction of sense of humour and degree of aggression on total adjustment, (4) interaction effect of sense of humour and inferiority feelings was not significant on the total adjustment of the individual, (5) interaction effect of inferiority feeling and degree of aggression on total adjustment was not significant, (6) there was no significant interaction effect among sense of humour, degree of aggression and inferiority feeling were also effective on emotional adjustment, (8) there was no significant effect of interaction of sense of humour and degree of aggression on the emotional adjustment of the individual, (9) there was no interaction effects of sense of humour and inferiority feelings on emotional adjustment, (10) there was a significant interaction effect of inferiority feeling and degree of aggression on emotional adjustment. The interaction effect of sense of humour degree of aggression and inferiority feeling on emotional adjustment was no significant, (11) the social adjustment of the individual was effected by the sense of humour and inferiority feelings, (12) aggression and social adjustment were unrelated, (13) there was no effect of sense of humour and degree of aggression on educational adjustment, (14) inferiority feeling was highly effective on educational adjustment, (15) there existed no interaction effect of degree of aggression, sense of humour and inferiority feeling on educational adjustment, (16) emotional adjustment, social adjustment and total adjustment were significantly related to sense of humour, (17) it was found that the inferiority feelings and total adjustment were significantly correlated, (18) all the three predicted variable, viz., sense of humour, degree of aggression and inferiority feelings contributed positively towards total adjustment. The same was true with emotional adjustment too, (19) for social adjustment only two variables, viz., inferiority feeling and sense of humour were found to be meaningful predictors.

Rawat (1995) studied the effect of parental absence on adjustment, study habits and academic development of student's of high school classes and found that: (1) the parent-present students differed significantly from the parent-absent students on their personality adjustment, while they did not differ on the study habits, except on comprehension and concentration dimension of study habits, (2) there was no significant difference between the two groups on their academic achievement.

Sinha and Singh (1995) studied adjustment as the factor of parent's aggression and strictness. They found that respondent's home adjustment was no influenced significantly either by their cultural background or by their parent's strictness. Respondents belonging to high aggressive parents showed poor adjustment. Forward caste's respondents showed better home adjustment to their backward counterparts irrespective of high and low aggressive/strict behaviour of their parents. On health adjustment it was found that respondents belonging to high aggressive parents faced more of health adjustment than their low counterparts. On social adjustment respondents, belonged to high aggressive parents showed poor social adjustment, parents strictness and castes of respondents did not influence social adjustment. On emotional adjustment respondents who belonged to high aggressive parents showed poor emotional adjustments that their low counterparts.

Bhardwaj (1997) undertook a psychosocial study of adjustment among adolescents. The objectives of the study were: to identify how far gender, mother's employment, extraversion and neuroticism play their role in influencing the adjustment of adolescent. The tools used to collect data included Junior Eysenck Personality Inventory by Helode and Adjustment Inventory by Mittla. The collected data were treated using mean, SD, *'t'* test and ANOVA. The major findings were: (1) Extraversion and neuroticism were found to have a powerful impact over global as well as area-wise (home, social, school, emotional and health) adjustment among adolescents, (2) Gender and mother's employment were not related to adolescent's global as well as area-wise adjustment, (3) It was found that global adjustment scores were influenced by the extraversion and neuroticism dimensions of personality, (4) The interaction effect were not found to be significant on any factor, (5) It was found that home adjustment was influenced by the extraversion and neuroticism dimensions of personality, (6) Extraversion, neuroticism and gender had significant effect on health and emotional adjustment.

STUDIES ON SELF-CONCEPT, ADJUSTMENT AND ACHIEVEMENT

A few scholars have tried to study the self-concept, adjustment and achievement simultaneously. In the following pages those studies are presented.

Goswami (1980) conducted a study on self-concept of adolescents and its relationship to scholastic achievement and adjustment.

The study was undertaken to achieve the following objectives: (1) to study the self-concept of the adolescents in relation to sex, intelligence and place of residence (rural-urban), (2) to find out the relationship between self-concept and scholastic achievement, (3) to find out the relationship between self-concept and adjustment.

In this study intelligence and adjustment were measured by administering: (i) Samanya Manasik Yogyata Parikash (A test of general mental·ability) by M.C. Joshi, and (ii) Vyaktitva Prakash Prashnavali by M.S.L. Saxena, respectively. Students marks obtained at the high school examination of U.P. Board (1976) served as an index of their scholastic achievement. A test of self-concept, Swatva-Bodh Parikshan was prepared by the investigator and used to find out the self-concept of the adolescents.

The major findings of the study were: (1) it was found that the global self-concept of the male adolescents was significantly different from that of the female adolescents and this difference was found both in the urban and rural population, (2) the sex difference was also found to be significant in respect of all the dimensions of self-concept as the male students had better global self-concept than the female adolescents, (3) a positive and significant correlation between self-concept and intelligence was found, (4) it was found that the difference between the means of the self-concept scores of the urban and rural adolescents was not significant, (5) it was found that a positive and significant correlation (P > .01) existed between global self-concept and scholastic achievement and also this relationship was positive and significant for male-female and urban rural sub-population of the adolescents, (6) a positive and significant correlation between self-concept and adjustment was found, but the correlation between the concept of intellectual ability and adjustment was not found to be significant for the sub-population of female adolescents.

Sharma (1983) undertook a study to ascertain the extent of influence of self-concept and adjustment on academic achievement. A sample of 1060 students, both boys and girls between the age of 13+ and 18+, was drawn by random sampling from classes X to XII belonging to various socio-economic strata. Data were collected from 18 educational institutions of eight towns of U.P. Only urban and semi-urban areas have been covered. The major conclusions were; (i) the self-concept affected academic achievement; (ii) the two areas of self-concept which had significant bearing on academic achievement were intellectual and school status and physical appearance and attributes; (iii) self-concept of intellectual and school status had been found to be conducive to high achievers whereas the self-concept of physical appearance and attributes had inverse relationship with academic achievement, (iv) adjustment did not influence academic achievement;

(v) differences in academic achievement had been found to influence certain measures of self-concepts but differences in academic achievement is not influence adjustment, and (vi) differences in adjustment influenced self-concept and vice-versa.

Gupta (1984) found that there was some relationship between self-concept, anxiety dependency and adjustment for the experimental group. Subjects reared in an artificial family atmosphere with surrogate mothers had better self-concept and adjustment with less anxiety than subjects reared in general homes without any substitute parents figure. Self-concept and adjustment were positively correlated and they had negative correlation anxiety.

The study of Pandit (1985) showed that: (i) there were significant difference between the ideal self and perceived self and ideal self and social self of adolescents, (ii) the difference between perceived self and social self was not significant, (iii) the adjustment of adolescents in home, health, social, emotional and school areas was significantly different in all cases except in the case of home and health adjustment, (iv) out of all five areas of adjustment the school adjustment was most satisfactory, followed by health, home, emotional, and social adjustment respectively, (v) the result for self-concept of adolescent boys and adolescent girls showed that boys had a higher regards for the attributes and qualities which they perceive as possessed by them, than girls, (vi) the study found that the social and emotional adjustment of adolescent boys was more satisfactory than that of adolescent girls.

Broderick (1992) examined the unique contributions of friendship and social acceptance to the development of the self and adjustment of preadolescents. The results of the study were:

Children with friends were found to have significantly more positive social perceptions of others than children without friends. There were no differences between the groups on general self-wroth. Children with friends were rated by their teachers as significantly less negative—aggressive and significantly less actively involved in classroom discussions than children without friends.

Popular children were found to exhibit significantly more extremely negative social perceptions than unpopular children. Popular children were rated by their teachers as significantly more active involved in classroom discussion and as significantly less socially withdrawn than unpopular children.

Sundararajan, Govindarajan and Rajasekar (1994) studied the self-concept and adjustment problems of B.Ed teacher-trainees. They found that, (i) the men teacher-trainees were found to be better than the women teacher-trainees in social adjustment and emotional adjustment, (2) the women teacher-trainees were better than men teacher-trainees in health adjustment, (3) the post-graduated teacher-trainees were seen to be better than their graduate counterparts in all areas of adjustment, except in health adjustment, (4) the teacher trainees of the humanities group were better in health adjustment, than the teacher-trainees of the science group, (5) the science teacher-trainees had more health problems than the teacher trainees of the humanities group, but they were better than the teacher-trainees of the humanities group in respect of the total and home adjustment, (6) the teacher-trainees with a high level of self-concept were better than their counterparts with a low level of self-concept in all the areas of adjustment, except the home area, where there was no significant difference.

AN APPRAISAL OF REVIEW

Research studies, either in India or abroad, quoted in the foregoing pages indicate that environmental structure of educational institutions, social and cultural factors might affect the growth and development of the self-concept, adjustment and achievement of the students. But research findings are not conclusive. Many investigators (Kurtz and Swenson, 1951, Nason, 1958; Davidson and Lang, 1960; Payne, 1962; Coopersmith, 1967; Vasanatha 1974; Wylie, 1974; Goswami 1980; Brookover, Patterson and Thomas, 1982; Sharma, 1983; and Shah, 1998) found a positive relationship between self-concept and achievement of secondary school students. It is found that high achievers in schools possess a feeling of adequacy. In these studies, some investigators have even found relatively low correlations between self-concept and achievement; others have found fairly high correlations, comparable with the correlations between aptitude test scores and academic achievement.

On the other hand, Mintz (1975) reported in his study that total self-concept was a poor predictor of achievement for the sixth grade students. Bruce and Howard (1977), Maikhuri and Pande (1997) reported that high School student's achievement was not related to their self-concept. At the adolescent level, Smith (1932) found that 'inferiority feeling' was as common among students with high ability as among students with low ability. In still another study at the high school level, Spivack (1956) found that there was a zero correlation between academic achievement and self-acceptance. Sharma (1970) suggested a curvilinear relationship between self-concept and school achievement.

Studies show that adjustment is a variable, still explorable, which have been studied in the context of various personality characteristics, intellectual and non-intellectual factors of pupils. Studies have found that adjustment is significantly related with school achievement (Bhatnagar, 1966 a and b; George and Abraham, 1967; Rajanankkam and Vasanthal, 1933; Rongali, 1993), Sex (Sharma, 1979; Mattoo, 1980; Tripathi, 1981; Swain and Panda, 1982; Sultana, 1983; Annama, 1984; Saraswat, 1986; Keshap, 1993; Sethi, 1993; Chouhan and Murthy, 1994), grade (Nomani, 1965; George, 1966; Goswami 1980), age (Pandey, 1970) residentialy (Pandey, 1979); Reddy and Sudha, 1980; Singh and Singh, 1987; Kasinath, 2000), Caste (Sharma, 1979, Kamlesh, 1981; Singh and Singh 1987; Kumar, Singh and Mohammed, 1995), Socio-economic status (Jogawar, 1976; Mattoo, 1980;Tripathi, 1981; Saraswat; 1982), parental attitude (Lata, 1985), family structure (Gupta 1981; Fox, 1990), family climate (Anshu, 1985), organizational climate (Kasinath, 2000), school typology (Kukreti, 1994; Sharma and Jakhar, 1999), academic streams (Agarwal and Sonawat, 1991; Kumar, Singh and Mohamad, 1995), occupational status (Rajanankkam and Vasanthal,

1993), level of aspiration (Pandey, 1979), creativity (Asha, 1978; Chaurasia, 1993), intelligence (Srivastaava, 1980), aggression (Chaurasia, 1993; Manju, 1994; Sinha and Singh, 1995), Locus of control (Sultana, 1983), study habits (Rawat, 1995), interest (Srivastava, 1980), physical disabilities (Kumar, Prasad and Prasad, 1995; Aminabhavi, 1996), extraversion and neuroticism (Bhardwaj, 1997), sense of humour (Manju, 1994), inferiority feeling (Manju, 1994), and self-concept (Goswami, 1980; Saraswat, 1982; Gupta, 1984).

Researchers have also found difference in high and low achievers in adjustment (Saun, 1980; Swain and Panda, 1982); Kapoor, 1987; Estridge 1989; Sethi, 1993, Chouhan and Murthy, 1984). On the other hand, no significant differences were noted by some researchers (Swain and Panda, 1982; Sharma 1983; Kalie and Kaur, 1995; Nair, 1999)

The foregoing review of the studies in the field of self-concept, adjustment and achievement as accomplished and reported in the Indian and Foreign context clearly reveal that so far no attempt (except Aggarwal and Sonawat, 1991; Kumar, Singh and Mohamad, 1995) has been made to study self-concept and adjustment across the academic streams. Further a few studies have been undertaken to compare the high and low achievers in terms of their self-concept and adjustment. The present investigation thus, embodies an attempt to probe and penetrate the fresh issues relating to an un-chartered territory in the domain of self-concept, adjustment and achievement.

Design of the Study

The first and most important requisite in any research is data without which no study could be conducted. Data are like raw materials without which no study could be conducted and hence production in research is not possible. For collection of data, the investigator has to set up the design, describe the sampling method, the population and the sample, the tools, used for collection of data, the reliability and validity of the tools used, the method adopted and the procedure employed in tabulation and organization of the data.

In this context, Mouly (1964) remarks "Scientific problem can be resolved only on the basis of data and major responsibility of the scientist is to set up a research design capable of providing the data necessary to the solution of his problem. While the unit of research makes it impossible to say that one aspect is more crucial than another, the collection of data is of paramount importance in the conduct of research, since obviously, no solution can be more adequate than the data on which it is based".

The previous chapter's review of related literature pertaining to the present investigation, precise formulation of the research problem, relevant hypotheses, etc., have been discussed. Keeping in view the above fact the researcher felt it very essential to describe the design of the study which includes a brief description of the method, population and sample, tools, data collection procedure and the statistical techniques. Employed in conducting the study at present.

METHOD OF THE STUDY

The study at present has been planned and implemented under a descriptive and cross-sectional framework. It aims at comparing the high and low academic achievers in their self-concept formation and adjustment. As such the ambit of the investigation was confined to a descriptive and analytical approach.

Hillway (1956) mentions, "If the scholar can not clearly describe his method, the chances are that it is too vague and general to yield him satisfactory results." So there is need to describe the method used in research work. The decision about the methods depends upon the nature of the problems selected, the kind of data necessary and its objectives. Keeping in view the above rationale the investigator has chosen the method for his study. Best (1978) states:

Descriptive research describes and interprets what is. It is concerned with conditions or relationships that exist; practices that prevail; beliefs, points of view of attitudes that are held; processes that are being felt; or trends that are developing.

Descriptive research goes beyond mere collection of data and tabulating them. It involves meaningful analysis of the data and drawing out the relevant inferences and significant conclusions. Hence, description of the investigation is obviously combined with analysis, comparison, contrast, interpretation, and evaluation.

Descriptive studies collect and provide three types of informations: (i) of what exists with respect to variables or conditions in a situations; (ii) of what we want by identifying standards or norms with which to compare the present conditions or what experts considered to be desirable; and (iii) of how to achieve goals by exploring possible ways and means on the basis of the experience of others or the opinion of experts.

The descriptive studies as in any study (i) identity and define their problem; (ii) state their objectives and hypotheses,

(iii) list the kind of data necessary and its objectives, keeping in view, the above rationale the investigator has chosen the method for his study. Best (1978) states:

Descriptive research describes and interprets what is. It is concerned with conditions or relationship that exist; practices that prevail; beliefs, points of view of attitudes that are held processes that are being felt; or trends that are developing.

Descriptive research goes beyond mere collection of data and tabulating them. It involves meaningful analysis of the data and drawn-out the relevant inferences and significant conclusions. Hence, description of the investigation is obviously combined with analysis, comparison, contrast, interpretation, and evaluation.

Descriptive studies collect and provide three types of information: (i) of what exists with respect to variables or conditions in a situation; (ii) of what we want by identifying standards or norms with which to compare the present conditions or what experts considered to be desirable; and (iii) of how to achieve goals by exploring possible ways and means on the basis of the experience of others or the opinion of experts.

The descriptive studies as in any study they (i) identify and define their problem; (ii) state their objectives and hypothesis; (iii) list the assumptions upon which their hypotheses and procedures are based; (iv) choose appropriate subjects and source materials; (v) select or construct tools for collecting data; (vi) specify categories of data that are relevant for the purpose of study, and capable of bringing out significant similarities, differences, or relationships; (vii) describe, analyze, and interpret their data in clear and precise terms; and (viii) draw significant and meaningful conclusions.

So far as the research methodology is concerned, the present study comes under the scope of "Descriptive Research". This is a status study of descriptive nature made on the basis of data gathered through field investigation. So the method, to be more exact, followed in this study was said to be the "Descriptive Survey" under "Causal Comparative" one.

This study would explore the causal relationship among samples those are different on the critical variable like self-concept, adjustment and academic achievement.

POPULATION AND SAMPLE

During recent years appropriate techniques for sampling have increasingly used in social sciences to get information necessary about a specific population because it is very difficult for an investigator to collect information about certain characteristics for the whole population (i.e., target population). Through appropriate sampling techniques, it is possible to draw a representative sample from the population so that the findings can safely be extended to the target population. In the present study the investigator had taken such steps as were necessary to see that the sampled population was representative of the target population.

All the students, irrespective of their academic streams, reading in higher secondary classes (i.e. 1st year) of undivided Koraput district of Orissa constituted the population of the study. The undivided Koraput district at present has been divided into four districts namely Koraput, Malkangiri, Nawrangpur and Rayagada. The reason for selecting the undivided Koraput district is that it is district having both tribal and non-tribal students. The study of these students can give some insight into their basic problems.

It was decided to have the higher secondary students (i.e., 1st year) as the subjects of the study, the reason of selecting Higher Secondary Students (i.e., 1st year) is that they have already passed the High School Certificate Examination which is uniform for all the students, more reliable data regarding their level of academic achievement can be obtained by analysing their marks secured in that examination.

To ensure the representativeness of the sample, the investigator adopted stratified random sampling technique. In stratified sampling, the population is first divided into two homogeneous or administratively convenient sub-populations or strata and from each stratum a separate sample of unit is selected (Srivastava and Bhatkulikar, 1980).

The main objective of the study was to compare the high and low achievers with regard to their self-concept and adjustment. The secondary objective was to study the self-concept and adjustment across the academic streams, sex and residence. Therefore, in the present study due representation has been given to academic stream, sex and residence.

Srivastava and Bhatkulikar (1980) and Verma (1966) have mentioned that sometimes an investigator deliberately selects samples of equal size or different sizes (but not necessarily proportional to stratum size) from the different strata. This is often done to increase the representation of very small strata in the total sample, or reduce the sample size in the case of large but homogeneous strata.

Thus, a two stage stratified disproportionate random sampling frame was adopted. The first stage of stratification pertained to the location of institutions. All institutions having higher secondary education facilities/provision in the undivided district of Koraput were stratified into urban and rural as per the list provided by the Deputy Secretary, CHSE, Berhampr, Jeypore Zone, Orissa.

In the second stage, these institutions were stratified in terms of management (i.e. government and private-Aided).

The total number of government and private-Aided institutions were 35 till the date of data collection. A list indicating the number of institutions in each category was then prepared. It was decided to take at least 600 students, spreaded equally over three academic streams (i.e., Arts, Science, and Commerce) for final analysis of the study. Thus from each academic stream a sample of 200 students spreaded over sex (i.e., male and female) and residence (i.e. urban and rural) was drawn randomly. Thus, the sample of the present study consisted of 600 students. Table 4.1 illustrates the total number of students spreaded over in terms of location, academic streams and sex.

A look at Table 4.1 shows that the number of institutions selected, the number of students from each academic stream, the number of rural and urban students and the number of male and female students forming part of the sample of the study are broadly representative. Thus, in all there are 300 urban students (i.e., 100 students from each stream), 300 rural students (i.e., 100 students from each stream), 300 male students (i.e., 100 male students from each stream), 300 female students (i.e., 100 female students from each stream) and 200 students from each academic stream which may be considered adequate for determining the representativeness of sample of students of the study.

TOOLS USED

The following data gathering instruments have been used in the present study to collect the data.

1. Self-concept questionnaire by Saraswat (1984).
2. Adjustment Inventory developed by Sinha and Singh (1993) (age group 14 to 18 years).
3. Scores of Academic Achievement.

A brief description of these tools have been given in the following discussion.

Self-Concept Questionnaire

Self-Concept Questionnaire standardized by Saraswat (1984) was used in this study to measure the self-concept of the students. The questionnaire is meant for higher secondary students. The self-concept Inventory provides six separate dimensions of self-concept, i.e., Physicial, Social, Intellectual, Moral, Educational and Temperamental self-concept. It also gives total self-concept score. The operational definitions of self-concept dimensions measured by this inventory are:

Table 4.1: Distribution of Sample Students into Different Categories

S. No.	*Name of the institution*	*Arts*		*Science*		*Commerce*	
		Male	*Female*	*Male*	*Female*	*Male*	*Female*
A. Urban							
1.	D.A.V. College, Koraput	20	15	20	15	15	10
2.	V.D. College, Jeypore	10	10	10	15	15	20
3.	Rayagada College, Rayagada	10	13	10	10	10	10
4.	Nawrangpur College, Nawrangpur	10	12	10	10	10	10
	Total	50	50	50	50	50	50
B. Rural							
1.	H.A.L., Sunabeda	10	15	15	15	10	15
2.	Semiliguda College, Semiliguda	10	05	10	10	05	10
3.	Laxmipur College, Laxmipur	05	05	NP	NP	NP	NP
4.	Umerkote College, Umerkote	05	05	05	05	10	08
5.	Malkangiri College, Malkangiri	05	05	NP	NP	10	08
6.	Balimela College, Balimela	05	05	10	10	NP	NP
7.	Gunpur College, Gunpur	05	05	05	05	15	09
8.	Padmapur College, Padmapur	05	05	05	05	NP	NP
	Total	50	50	50	50	50	50

NP: No provision.

Physical

Individuals view of their body, health physical appearance and strength.

Social

Individuals' sense of worth in social interactions.

Temperamental

Individuals' view of their prevailing emotional state or predominance of a particular kind of emotional reaction.

Educational

Individuals' view of themselves in relation to school, teachers and extracurricular activities.

Moral

Individuals' estimation of their moral worth; right and wrong activities.

Intellectual

Individuals' awareness of their intelligence and capacity of problem solving and judgments.

Table 4.2 indicates item numbers included in different self-concept dimensions.

Table 4.2: Self-concept Dimensions along with their Item Numbers

Self-concept dimensions	*Code No.*	*Item numbers*
Physical	A	2, 3, 9, 20, 22, 27, 29, 31
Social	B	1, 8, 21, 37, 40, 43, 46, 48
Temperamental	C	4, 10, 14, 16, 19, 23, 24, 28
Educational	D	5, 13, 15, 17, 25, 26, 30, 32
Moral	E	6, 34, 35, 41, 42, 44, 45, 47
Intellectual	F	7, 11, 12, 18, 33, 36, 38, 39

The Inventory contains 48 items. Each dimension contains eight items. Each item is provided with five alternatives. Responses are obtained on the test booklet itself. There is no time limit but generally 25 minutes have been found sufficient for responding all the items.

Reliability of the Self-Concept Questionnaire

Reliability of the Inventory was found by test-retest method, and it was found to be 0.91 for the total self-concept measures. Reliability co-efficient of its various dimensions vary from 0.67 to 0.88. Table 4.3 shows the test-retest reliability for each dimension.

Table 4.3: Test-Retest Reliability of the Self-concept Inventory

Code No.	*Self-concept Dimension*	*No. of Items*	*Reliability Co-efficient*
A	Physical	8	0.77
B	Social	8	0.83
C	Temperamental	8	0.79
D	Educational	8	0.88
E	Moral	8	0.67
F	Intellectual	8	0.79
	Total self-concept	48	0.91

Validity of the Self-concept Questionnaire

Expert-s opinion were obtained to establish the validity of the inventory. Hundred items were given to 25 Educationalists to classify the items to the category to which it belongs. Items of highest agreement and not less than 80% of agreement were selected. Thus the content and construct validity were established.

Standardization and Norms

The Self-concept Questionnaire was standardized on 1000 students of 20 Higher Secondary Schools of Delhi pertaining to Delhi Administration and Central Schools. The students were from IXth and XIth classes ranging from 14 to 18 years of both the sexes.

Table 4.4: Interpretation and Classification of Raw Scores for all Dimensions

Self-Concept Dimension Scores	*Interpretation (Category)*
33 to 40	High self-concept
25 to 32	Above average concept
17 to 24	Average concept
9 to 16	Below average concept
Upto 8	Low concept

Table 4.5: Interpretation and Classification of Raw Scores for Total Self-Concept

Raw Score	*Interpretation*
193 to 240	High self-concept
145 to 192	Above average concept
97 to 144	Average concept
49 to 96	Below average concept
1 to 48	Low concept

Instructions for Administering the Inventory

1. Proper seating arrangement of the students were taken care of.
2. Before the starting of the test, the students were properly instructed to keep their books and notebooks aside or inside the desks.
3. It was made sure that the respondent had a pencil or pen.
4. The students were told clearly the purpose of the test.
5. The students were assured that the responses obtained on the test would be kept secret.

6. Any doubts raised by the students were answered frankly.
7. The test-booklets of self-concept inventory were distributed to the students.
8. The students were instructed to fill up the entries of the responses one-by-one.
9. The instructions from the test booklets were rade clearly while the individuals were reading silently.
10. It was ensured that the instructions had been understood correctly by them.
11. Doubts and queries were invited. Such doubts were clarified before they start responding the items.
12. To make sure that all were responding in a desired way they were properly supervised.
13. If some one was needing to know the meaning of certain words he was told. The responses had been decided independently by the candidates themselves.
14. At the end of the testing the test booklets were counted and it was made sure that all the test booklets had been returned.

Instruction to Students

Read the following instructions from the inventory in English.

"This is a self-concept inventory. There are 48 items in it. Against each item, there are five responses. You have to read each item carefully and respond to it by marking a tick (√) on any one of the five responses given against that item, which you think appropriate for you.

There is no right or wrong answer. The right answer is only what you feel about yourself. Try to give your responses according to what you feel about yourself with reference to that statement. Your answers will be kept confidential.

After the above instructions the researcher had explained the example given on the inventory.

Scoring Method

The respondent had been provided with five alternatives to give his responses ranging from most acceptable to least acceptable description of his self-concept. The alternatives or responses were arranged in such a way that the scoring system for all the items will remain the same i.e., 5, 4, 3, 2, 1 whether the items are positive or negative. If the respondent put (√) mark for first alternative the score is '5', for second alternative the score is '4', for third alternative score is '3' for the fourth it is '2' and for the fifth and last alternative the score is one. The summated score of all the forty-eight items provide the total self-concept score of an individual. A high score on this inventory indicates a higher self-concept, while a low score shows low self-concept. The score of each item had been transferred on the front page against that item. All the scores of eight items given in that column were added and it gives score for that particular dimension of self-concept.

Adjustment Inventory

Adjustment Inventory standardized by Sinha and Singh (1993) was used in this study to measure the adjustment of the subject. The adjustment inventory has been designed to measure the adjustment pattern in the three areas of adjustment, i.e., Emotional, Social, and Educational with in the age group from 14 to 18 years. This inventory consists of 60 items in total and 20 items in each area of adjustment.

Reliability of the Inventory

Coefficient of reliability was determined by:

(i) Split-half method,

(ii) Test-retest method, and

(iii) K.R. formula-20.

Table 4.6 gives the reliability co-efficient of the total test and of sub-tests by different methods.

Table 4.6: Reliability Coefficient of the Adjustment Inventory

Method used	*Emotional*	*Social*	*Educational*	*Total*
1. Split-half	0.94	0.93	0.96	0.95
2. Test-retest	0.96	0.90	0.93	0.93
3. K.R. Formula-20	0.92	0.92	0.96	0.94

Validity of the Inventory

In item-analysis validity coefficients were determined for each item by biserial correlation method and only such items were retained which yielded biserial correlation with both the criteria (i) total score and (ii) area score, significant level being .001.

Inter-correlation's among the three areas of the inventory were calculated. The correlation matrix is being presented in Table 4.7.

Table 4.7: Correlation Matrix of the Three Areas of Adjustment

	Areas	I	II	III
(i)	Emotional	—	.20	.19
(ii)	Social	.20	—	.24
(iii)	Educational	.19	.24	—

The Inventory was also validated by correlating inventory scores with ratings by the Hostel Superintendent. This was done on the data of 60 pupils living in the hostel of Patna Collegiate Multipurpose Higher Secondary School. The Hostel Superintendent rated the pupils on a five-point scale, namely, Excellent, Good, Average, Poor, and Very Poor in respect of their adjustment. The product moment coefficient of correlation between inventory scores and superintendent's rating was obtained to be 0.51.

Norms

Percentile norms were computed for both males and females of all the three areas (Emotional, Social and

Educational) of adjustment separately as also for the whole inventory. Table 4.8 and Table 4.9 gives the percentiles for male and females respectively.

Table 4.8: Percentile Norms for Males

Percentiles	*Emotional*	*Social*	*Educational*	*Total*
P_{90}	9.98	9.98	9.95	26.89
P_{80}	9.10	9.16	9.11	23.41
P_{70}	8.11	8.24	8.34	21.34
P_{60}	7.21	7.38	7.40	19.36
P_{50}	6.18	6.58	6.48	17.34
P_{40}	5.91	6.00	5.98	16.06
P_{30}	4.42	4.91	4.82	14.32
P_{20}	3.11	3.75	3.33	11.77
P_{10}	2.01	2.70	2.02	8.82

Table 4.9: Percentile Norms for Females

Percentiles	*Emotional*	*Social*	*Educational*	*Total*
P_{90}	9.80	9.91	9.95	27.67
P_{80}	8.31	8.45	8.81	23.89
P_{70}	7.45	7.55	7.67	21.63
P_{60}	6.88	6.91	6.98	19.40
P_{50}	6.12	6.27	6.31	17.78
P_{40}	5.11	5.62	5.73	16.15
P_{30}	4.21	4.31	4.62	14.53
P_{20}	3.11	3.08	3.61	11.81
P_{10}	2.00	2.31	2.71	8.70

The subjects can be classified into five categories in accordance with the raw scores obtained by them on the inventory. The five different categories of adjustment are, 'A' which stands for excellent, 'B' which stands for good, 'C' which stands for average, 'D' which stands for unsatisfactory, and

'E' which stands for very unsatisfactory adjustments. This categorization was done by dividing the base line of the normal curve into five equal units, each unit being equal to 1.2, Table 4.10 presents the classification of adjustment for total-score and Table 4.11 shows the classification in respect of the three areas: Emotional, Social and Educational.

Table 4.10: Classification of Adjustment in Terms of Categories

Category	*Description*	*Range of Score*	
		Male	*Female*
A	Excellent	5 and below	5 and below
B	Good	6-12	6-14
C	Average	13-21	15-22
D	Unsatisfactory	22-30	23-31
E	Very unsatisfactory	above	32 and above

Table 4.11: Classification of Adjustment in terms of Categories in the Three Areas

Area	*Category*	*Description*	*Ranges of Score*	
			Male	*Female*
Emotional	A	Excellent	1 and below	1 and below
	B	Good	2-4	2-5
	C	Average	5-7	6-7
	D	Unsatisfactory	8-10	8-10
	E	Very unsatisfactory	11 and above	11 and above
Social	A	Excellent	2 and below	3 and below
	B	Good	3-4	3-5
	C	Average	5-7	6-7
	D	Unsatisfactory	8-10	8-10
	E	Very unsatisfactory	11 and above	11 and above

Educational	A	Excellent	2 and below	2 and below
	B	Good	3-4	3-4
	C	Average	5-7	5-7
	D	Unsatisfactory	8-10	8-10
	E	Very unsatisfactory	11 and above	11 and above

Table 4.12 gives Mean and S.Ds. of the population upon which norms are based.

Table 4.12: Mean and SDs. of the Population upon which Norms are Based

Area	*Males*		*Female*	
	Mean	*S.D.*	*Mean*	*S.D.*
Emotional	5.62	3.12	6.55	2.81
Social	5.91	2.38	6.21	2.52
Educational	6.38	2.91	5.35	3.00
Total	17.91	7.36	18.11	7.27

Meaning of the symbols and explanation of the areas.

(i) Emotional Adjustment

High scores indicate unstable emotion. Students with low sources tend to be emotionally stable.

(ii) Social Adjustment

Individuals scoring high are submissive and retering, low scores indicate aggressive behaviour.

(iii) Educational Adjustment

Individuals scoring high are poorly adjusted with their curricular and co-curricular programmes. Persons with low scores are interested in school programmes.

Instructions for Test Users

1. It is a self-administering inventory. Therefore the instructions were given to the testees to read the test silently.

2. There is no time limit for answering it; ordinarily an individual takes 15 minutes in completing the test.

3. The researcher had instructed the students to interpret the meaning of the sentences themselves. However, meaning of the difficult words asked by the students were told.

4. Co-operation of the examinees were sought in answering the inventory and the examinees were assured that their answers and scores will be treated with strictest confidence.

5. The researcher had indicated frankly and honestly the purpose of the test when any question regarding this was raised by the exmainees.

6. There was no need of telling why letters and numbers are placed before the questions. If a question was asked about these, the researcher had told the meaning of the letters.

Instructions for Scoring

Inventory can be scored by hand only. For any answer indicative of adjustment zero is given, otherwise a score of one is awarded. Table 4.13 shows the key responses indicative of lack of adjustment.

Scores of Academic Achievement

No specific test was used to assess the academic achievement of the subjects by the investigator. It was decided to take the total marks secured by the subjects in the Annual H.S.C. Examination 1999 conducted by the Board of Secondary Education, Orissa for the purpose. Many investigators have used the school marks for determining the academic achievement. Sharma (1968) found the reliability and validity of the school marks as a satisfactory measure for use in research studies. Passi (1971) used the school achievement scores in school subjects taking the percentage of aggregate marks obtained in the middle standard examination.

Table 4.13: Key Responses Indicative of Lack of Adjustment

Emotional		*Social*		*Educational*	
Item No.	*Response indicative of lack of adjustment*	*Item No.*	*Response indicative of lack of adjustment*	*Item No.*	*Response indicative of lack of adjustment.*
1	Yes	2	Yes	3	Yes
4	Yes	5	Yes	6	Yes
7	Yes	8	Yes	9	Yes
10	Yes	11	No	12	No
13	Yes	14	Yes	15	Yes
16	Yes	17	No	18	No
19	Yes	20	No	21	Yes
22	Yes	23	No	24	No
25	Yes	26	No	27	Yes
28	Yes	29	Yes	30	No
31	Yes	32	No	33	No
34	Yes	35	Yes	36	Yes
37	Yes	38	No	39	Yes
40	Yes	41	No	42	Yes
43	Yes	44	No	45	Yes
46	Yes	47	Yes	48	No
49	Yes	50	No	51	No
52	Yes	53	No	54	No
55	Yes	56	No	57	No
58	Yes	59	No	60	No

On those ground it was decided not to make use of any specific achievement test in the present study but to use the total marks secured by the students in the Annual H.S.C. Examination, 1999.

COLLECTION OF DATA

The subjects of the present study were selected from the prescribed population. Names of the institutions, number of subjects across locality, academic stream and sex etc. Have already been given in Table 4.1. The principals of these institutions were approached one-by-one and the purpose of the study was explained. Almost all the principals provided the facilities for collection of data. The data and time of data collection was fixed on the basis of the advice and convenience of each institution. The selected students of each institution were assembled in one room to take test. Necessary rapport was established through personal contacts. The purpose of the study was explained to them. The sampled subjects were first administered the self-concept questionnaire (Saraswat, 1984; c.f. Appendix A-1). They were requested to answer all the questions, sincerely and frankly. They were assured that the responses would be kept strictly confidential. They took about 25 minutes to complete the self-concept questionnaire. After a short interval of 20 minutes Adjustment Inventory (Sinha and Singh, 1993) c.f. Appendix A-2 was administered to them. Necessary instructions were given to them. Attempts were made to elicit free responses. They took about 15 minutes to complete the inventory.

They were further requested to write their percentage of marks secured in the last 1999 H.S.C. Examination conducted by B.S.E., Orissa at the top of the first page of the answer sheet. In order to verify the correctness of the marks of each subject, they were told to give a Xerox copy of the mark sheet of H.S.C. Examination 1999.

The completed response sheet of each student was scored manually according to the instructions given for the scoring procedure in the test manuals. After scoring all the tests investigator organized the whole data, checked it to see the accuracy, utility and completeness. After editing, the data were classified and tabulated for its analysis according to the objectives of the study (c.f. Appendices B_1, B_2 and B_3). The data were organized on master charts separately for computer analysis.

DATA TREATMENT

The main purpose of the study was to compare the self-concept and adjustment of high and low achievers. The data obtained on academic achievement were tabulated into frequency distribution and then p 75 and P 25 were calculated for identifying the high achievers and low achievers respectively.

The data obtained on self-concept, and adjustment for urban and rural, each stream and male and females were tabulated separately into frequency distributions. Mean scores and SDs of each group on self-concept and adjustment were computed. Frequency distributions for all the groups were approximately normal. Hence the comparison between different groups was made on the basis of the '*t*'-test with 0.05 and 0.01 levels of confidence considered significant.

In order to find out the relationship among the three variables (i.e., self-concept, adjustment, and achievement), the data were got analyzed through the computer.

Self-Concept of Students: An Analysis

Self-concept has been reckoned as a potent means for making a deep study of personality as it helps in understanding human behaviour. It is now believed that 'self' is a principal controlling agent which shapes human destiny. In reality, 'self' is viewed by the majority of self-psychologists as the nucleus of human body.

Thus, the self is not only related to motivational activity alone, but acts as a regulating and co-ordinating factor in perceiving, learning, remembering, planning, risk taking, judging and in decision taking matters or situations. While solving a problem or in undertaking some work, the level of performance is determined not only by the difficulty or ease of the problem, but also by the image one has built about oneself in general. When one grows, one learns about one's reciprocities with others as high, low, friendly, dominant or subordinate.

This chapter presents an analysis of self-concept of sampled students across their sex, residential background, academic streams and levels of achievement.

TESTING THE NORMALCY OF DISTRIBUTION OF THE SELF-CONCEPT SCORES

The first and third objectives of the investigation were to study the self-concept of the students across their sex, residential background and academic streams; and levels of achievement respectively. For the purpose a total sample of

600 students were administered the self-concept Questionnaire (SCQ) developed by Saraswat (1984). The distribution of scores on self-concept (i.e., dimension-wise and total) for the male, female, urban, rural, arts, science, commerce students along with high and low achievers were examined in respect of their nature and departure from normalcy. The assumption of normality is that the dependent variable in the population from which the samples have been drawn should be normally distributed. To be sure of the satisfaction of this assumption indices of Skewness and Kurtosis were computed following the percentile method (Garrett, 1971). Table 5.1 shows the findings in this regard.

The values of Skewness and Kurtosis (vide, Table 5.1) for all the dependent variables, except a few ones, indicated near normality. Boneau (1960) says:

That in a large number of research situations, the probability statements resulting from the use of *'t'* and *'f'* tests, even when these two assumptions of homogeneity and normality assumptions of homogeneity are violated will be highly accurate.

In the light of the remarks given above it was decided to use *'t'* test for all the variables.

SEX AND SELF-CONCEPT

Sex is considered to be an important variable in determining one's self-concept. Although scholars like Goswami (1978), Shah (1978), Desai (1979), Hirunval (1980), Saraswat (1982) have found significant sex differences in self-concept, still there are some studies which have pointed out no sex difference in self-concept, (Pandit 1969; De Blassie and Healy, 1970; Shah, 1978; Naval et al., and 1989).

In the light of these inconsistent findings the investigator was interested to find out the difference, if any, between the male and female students in their self-concept comparison between the two groups was made on the basis of the *'t'* test with 0.05 and 0.01 levels of confidence for significance. The relevant results are summarized in Table 5.2.

Table 5.1: Values of Skewness and Kurtosis of Self-concept (i.e., dimension-wise and total)

Sl.	Measures	Male		Female		Urban		Rural		Science		Arts		Commerce		High		Low	
No.	of self-concept	Sk	Ku	Sk	Ku	Sk	Ku	Sk	Ku	Sk	Ku	Sk	Ku	Sk	Ku	Sk	Ku	Sk	Ku
1.	Self-Concept (total)	–1.37	0.25	–1.42	0.32	–1.51	0.27	–1.36	0.31	–0.98	0.23	–0.79	0.18	0.41	0.27	0.17	0.35	–1.74	0.31
2.	Physical self-concept	0.14	0.16	0.32	0.25	0.27	0.16	0.28	0.15	0.17	0.21	0.021	0.17	0.23	0.31	0.24	0.21	0.17	0.28
3.	Social self-concept	–0.72	0.27	–0.63	0.31	–0.59	0.19	–0.73	0.21	0.20	0.24	0.18	0.32	0.26	–0.61	0.23	0.25	0.25	0.21
4.	Temperamental self-concept	–1.51	0.26	–1.25	0.15	–1.62	0.12	–1.58	0.27	-0.92	0.25	0.16	0.16	0.22	–0.72	0.18	–0.74	–1.92	0.27
5.	Educational self-concept	–1.78	0.04	–1.62	0.17	–1.68	007	–1.32	0.09	-1.56	0.07	–1.25	0.09	–1.65	0.08	–1.41	0.14	–2.15	0.21
6.	Moral self-concept	0.29	0.18	0.612	0.23	0.34	0.119	0.30	0.27	-0.72	0.11	–0.68	0.10	0.78	0.06	–0.09	0.11	0.32	0.17
7.	Intellectual self-concept	-1.86	0.23	–1.65	0.27	–1.71	0.24	–1.61	0.21	0.31	0.18	0.17	0.21	0.27	0.20	0.33	0.20	0.33	0.19

Table 5.2: Significance of Difference Between the Means of Self-Concept Scores for Male and Female Students

Sl. No.	*Measures of self-concept*	*Male students N = 300*		*Female students N = 300*		*SED*	*t-value*
		Mean	*SD*	*Mean*	*SD*		
1.	Physical (A)	29.3	3.92	28.05	3.99	.32	3.99**
2.	Social (B)	28.06	4.24	30.52	3.74	.33	7.45**
3.	Temperamental (C)	29.51	4.00	29.35	3.48	0.30	0.53
4.	Educational (D)	30.2	5.3	29.27	5.83	0.45	2.07*
5.	Moral (E)	30.57	4.71	31.74	4.11	0.36	3.25**
6.	Intellectual (F)	26.6	4.51	25.34	4.3	0.36	3.5**
7.	Total	174.24	17.81	174.34	16.75	1.41	.07

*$p < .05$.

**$p < .01$.

The statistical analysis (vide, Table 5.2) revealed that male and female students differed significantly in respect of their mean scores on five dimensions of self-concept (physical, $t = 3.91, p < .05$; Social $t = 7.45, p < .01$; educational $t = 2.07, p < .05$; moral $t = 3.25, p < .01$; and intellectual, $t = 3.50, p < .01$). On the basis of the comparison of their mean scores it can be concluded that male students appeared to have greater magnitude of physical, educational and intellectual self-concepts than their female counterparts. On the other hand, female students showed superiority over male students with regard to social and moral self-concepts. However, in case of temperamental dimension of self-concept and total self-concept the differences were not large enough to be declared statistically significant. Hence male and female students were found to be alike with regard to their temperamental and total self-concept. In view of the above results, the null hypothesis stating no significant sex differences in the self-concept (i.e., H-1) was retained in case of temperamental and total self-concept and on rest of the self-concepts it was rejected.

Results reported above indicate that sex does not emerge as an important determinant of self-concept of sampled students. It implies that both the male and female students occupied the similar position in their self-concept may be because they might perceive the situation in the similar way. It clarified that in the modern techno-scientific age, the self-concept status of male and female students is more or less similar. Because today, both males and females are equal in their social status and social prestige. The result of the study is in agreement with those of Pandit (1969), DeBlassie and Healy (1970), Shah (1978), Nayal et al. (1989). Who concluded that sex does not affect the self-concept of students. However, some other researchers like Goswami (1978), Sharma (1978), Desi (1979), Hirunval (1980), Saraswat (1982) had found sex differences in self-concept which contradict the present finding.

However, significant differences between male and female students were noted on five dimensions of self-concept (i.e., physical, social, educational, moral and intellectual). Male students exhibited superiority over female students with reference to physical, educational and intellectual dimensions of self-concept. It implies that the male students think more about their appearance, perceive themselves in doing physical work, value their personality and health. Besides they have positive attitude towards school studies and feel for doing home work assignment regularly, think about their teachers, believe in school examination together with regularly in the class attendance. They further think that they can discover something new if opportunities are given; careful before doing some work and try to solve their problems of studies intelligently. It is quite obvious. The present era witnessed competition. To compete with others are requires intelligence. Perhaps male students fall prey of competitions because of the social obligations. It is their belief that through intelligence excellence in education can be achieved. Since achievement and intelligence are related (i.e., empirically established) they want to do school works, sincerely, attend school regularly and face examination boldly, with the help of intelligence. For all these, they believe in their physical attributes. It is often said that sound mind lies in a sound body. So the male students value their physique etc., and its related dimensions. No parallel study is available to support or contradict the findings of the study but the study of Goswami (1990) found that male adolescents had better global self-concept than the female-adolescents.

It is interesting to note that the female students were superior to male students with regard to social and moral self-concepts. It highlights that the female students are very friendly, could express their ideas frankly before others, like the company of others, take part in organizing picnic. They do not hesitate in mixing with persons of opposite sex and to the work keeping in mind the desire of others. Further they believe in religious customs and traditions, perceive speaking of truth, obeying public rules and perceive moral character more important. They are quite aware of their right and wrong activities. In the Indian cultural matrix this trend is not surprising. Truxam and Merrill (1947) express the importance of culture as "a complete understanding of family depends upon viewing it in relation to its cultural setting. Relative importance of each of the family functions depends upon the total cultural configuration". Culture affects family form and division of authority. Each culture has its own norms which combine and make up the ethos of the group. Tiwari (1979) says that cultural settings has the most significant effect on all dimensions of parent-child relations, i.e., acceptance-rejection, dominance-submission, encouragement-discouragement love-hate, democracy-authoritarianism, trust-distrust, reward-punishment and tolerance-hostility in almost all situations.

In contemporary Indian culture, the primary functions of the family are socialization of the child and giving recognition. The foundations of socialization of the child is laid by the parents. Faith in God, even in science, individualism, ideological freedom, social customs, traditions, moral character, equality, fraternity, cooperation, fellow-feeling etc., are the outstanding features of the Indian society. Both men and women enjoy equal status in all spheres of life. Status of women is assured. For all these reasons female students might have more social and moral self-concepts. This finding is supported by Saraswat (1982) who reported that girls were higher on physical, social and moral self-concept.

Graphical representation of data was also attempted in Figure 1 which displays variance in the self-concept of male and female students. A cursory look on the bar diagram would suggest that the male students possess more physical, temperamental, educational, and intellectual self-concepts while female students had more of social and moral self-concepts.

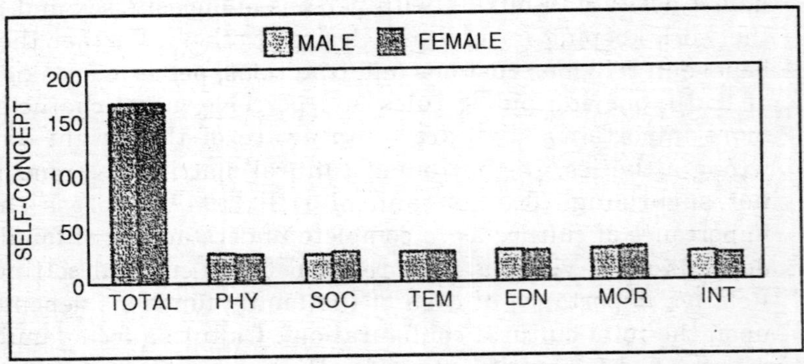

Fig. 1.: Bar Diagram Showing Mean Scores of Self-concept for Male and Female Students.

RURAL/URBAN BACKGROUND AND SELF-CONCEPT

Another important factor examined in relation to self-concept is the students' rural-urban background. There are empirical evidences (Goswami, 1980 and Singh, 1987) and logical grounds to presume that rural-urban origin has an association with the self-concept. Contrary to this observation some studies (Silverman, 1978; Saxena, 1981) have suggested that there is no difference in the self-concept between the rural and urban students.

In view of the above contradictory findings the investigator was interested to find out the difference, if any, between the rural and urban students in their self-concept. In this connection the hypothesis maintains that there is no significant difference in the self-concept (i.e., dimension-wise and total) of rural and urban students. Table 5.3 presents statistics pertaining to the significance of difference between means of self-concept for groups of students as per their residential background.

Table 5.3: Significance of Difference Between the Means of Self-concept Scores for Rural and Urban Students

Sl. No.	*Measures of self-concept*	*Urban N = 300*		*Rural N = 300*		*SED*	*t-value*
		Mean	*S.D.*	*Mean*	*S.D.*		
1.	Physical (A)	28.71	4.1	28.64	3.91	0.33	0.21
2.	Social (B)	28.73	4.53	29.86	3.71	0.35	3.23**
3.	Temperamental (C)	29.49	3.93	29.36	3.57	0.30	0.43
4.	Educational (D)	30.3	5.27	29.18	5.84	0.45	2.49*
5.	Moral (E)	31.38	4.71	30.93	4.21	0.36	1.25
6.	Intellectual (F)	26.59	4.45	25.35	4.41	0.36	3.43**
7.	Total	175.2	18.07	173.32	16.91	1.43	1.31

*$p < .05$.

** $p < .01$.

It is evident from Table 5.3 that significant differences existed in mean scores of students belonging to rural and urban areas with respect to their social (t = 3.23, $p < .01$), educational (t = 2.49, $p < .05$), and intellectual (t = 3.44, $p < .01$) dimensions of self-concept. Means shown in Table 5.3 indicate that urban students had higher magnitude of educational and intellectual self-concepts as compared to that of their rural counterparts. On the other hand rural students showed superiority over urban students. With regard to social self-concept. However in case of physical, temperamental, moral dimensions of self-concept and total self-concept the differences were not large enough to be declared statistically significant. Hence it can be said that rural and urban students were found to be similar with regard to their physical, temperamental moral and total self-concepts (cf., Fig. 2).

Hence the null hypothesis (i.e., H-2) was partly accepted and partly rejected.

The results pertaining to the comparison of self-concept of the students with regard to their residential background indicate that the difference between the means of the self-concept scores of the urban and rural adolescents was not significant. It is a general belief that urban students possess more self-concept than rural students. This belief was shattered on the basis of the present finding. Due to exposure to many situations of life and wider contact through mass-media the rural students have developed their perception of life, world etc. This is the age of information-technology. Information is no more the monopoly of the urban habitants. It has cut across the areas and reached the remote habitants. The score of viewing the world has been enlarged on which has, in turn, an impact on the individual's perception. Such a situation might narrowed down the age old gap that existed between the urban and rural students in their self-concept. Besides, parental awareness, encouragement, wider opportunities to learn to live in world community can be attributed to this situation. Such result contradicts the findings of Goswami (1980, Singh, (1987).

However, on the individual dimensions of the self-concept the urban rural differences were significant. The

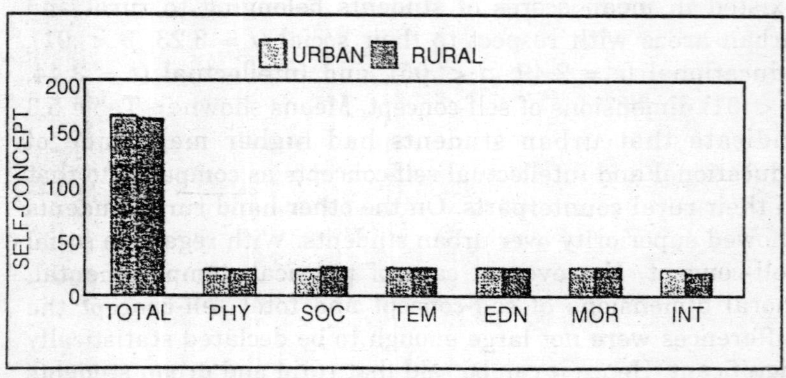

Fig. 2: Bar Diagram Showing Mean Scores of Self-concept for Urban and Rural Students.

urban students had better educational and intellectual self-concepts than their rural counterparts.

Such a finding seems to be justified. Generally urban students are from well-to-do families. The researchers have established that students belonging to the families with high socio-economic status were found to have significantly higher self-concept Gupta (1980) reported that students belonging to high socio-economic status had significantly higher perceived real self-concepts as compared to the students with low socio-economic status. Similarly, Jogawar (1976) found that better socio-economic status of adolescents helped then to develop their self-concept.

There is likelihood of interaction between socio-economic status, intelligence, environment and self-concept. Self-concept is a person's total subjective environment and a distinctive centre of experience and significance which results from the evaluational interaction with others becoming the consistent personal perspective of 'I' and 'Me' (Jewrsild et al., 1975). It includes cognitive components (i.e., an individuals' perception of this physical attributes and self-conceptions of himself, his abilities, purposes, beliefs, moral commitments and values); affective components (i.e., feelings, sentiments, moods); capacity for self-evaluation (i.e., approval or disapproval); and attitudinal components. All these components reacts with each other in a complex manner in different situations to give uniqueness and direction to human personality and behaviours. According to Shavelson et al., (1976) the construct of self-concept is linked with achievement and whether used as an outcome itself or as a moderator variable that helps explain achievement outcomes, is a critical variable in education and in educational evaluation and research.

The general which that rural students possess poor self-concepts stands falsified because they had better social self-concept than the urban students. The rural environment is found to be congenial for the development of social self-concept. The age-old Indian traditions, customs, rituals etc., are yet caught by the rural students, perhaps these are the determining force of their behaviour. The Indian village life embraces a very typical, unique form of living. In spite of the impact of modern science and technology the rural students had a strong perception for fellow-feeling, self-sacrifice and social interactions.

ACADEMIC STREAM AND SELF-CONCEPT

Another factor examined in relation to self-concept is the respondents' field of study (i.e., academic stream). A very few studies like Deo and Gupta, 1963; Nayal et al., 1989 have been conducted in this direction. An attempt has been made here to compare the self-concept of higher secondary students belonging to three different academic streams, namely, science, arts and commerce. It was hypothesized that there would be no significant difference in the self-concept (i.e., dimensions-wise and total) of: (a) arts and science students, (b) arts and commerce students, and (c) science and commerce students. In order to test this hypothesis comparisons were made between arts and science students, between arts and commerce students and between science and commerce students on self-concept as measured by SCQ (Saraswat, 1984). The scores obtained by arts, science and commerce students on six dimensions of self-concept, namely physical, social, temperamental, educational, moral and intellectual and total were tabulated separately into frequency distributions. Mean and SDs for each group on six scales and on total scale were calculated. Comparison among the groups were made on the basis of the '*t*'-test (i.e., two-tailed) with 0.05 level and 0.01 level of confidence for significance. The relevant results are summarised in Table 5.4 through 5.6.

A close perusal of Table 5.4 revealed significance of difference between arts and science students on educational ($t = 4.86$, $p < .01$) and intellectual ($t = 3.49$, $p < .01$) dimensions of self-concept. This suggests that arts and science students differed significantly with respect to their educational and intellectual self-concepts. On the basis of the comparison of their mean scores (cf. Fig. 3) it can be said that arts students had more educational and intellectual self-concepts. Hence the null hypothesis (i.e., 3a) was rejected with regard to foregoing two dimensions of self-concept. This result

Table 5.4: Comparison of Arts and Science Students on Self-concept

Sl. No.	*Measures of self-concept*	*Arts N = 200*		*Science N = 200*		*SED*	*t-value*
		Mean	*S.D.*	*Mean*	*S.D.*		
1.	Physical (A)	28.65	4.03	29.07	3.45	0.37	1.14
2.	Social (B)	28.75	4.35	29.34	3.47	0.39	1.51
3.	Temperamental (C)	29.76	4.02	29.59	3.63	0.39	0.44
4.	Educational (D)	32.52	4.25	30.14	5.43	0.49	4.86**
5.	Moral (E)	31.53	5.07	31.82	3.93	0.46	0.63
6.	Intellectual (F)	27.06	3.95	25.63	4.15	0.41	3.49**
7.	Total	178.26	17.66	175.59	17.68	1.77	1.51

** $p < .01$.

seems to be quite surprising because it has been generally observed that science students perceive more about their intelligence and education. The content of science is relatively more difficult and requires more attention of the students while they learn. They feel that they can learn the most by sharing ideas and talents, or by interacting with teachers and peers. They attend classes regularly and like more to work with others. Science students take the responsibility for

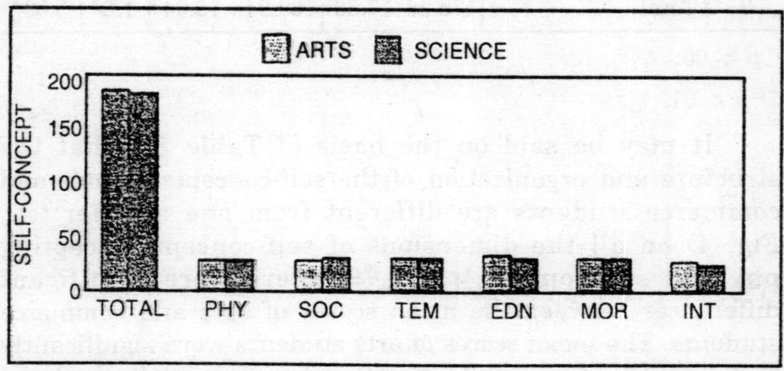

Fig. 3. Bar Diagram Showing Mean Scores of Self-concept for Arts and Science Students.

getting the most out of the class and participate with others when to do so. The present finding might have emerged because of the small number of subjects was included in the study. However, these two groups did not differ significantly on physical, social, temperamental and moral dimensions of self-concept and on total self-concept too. Here the null hypothesis anticipating no significant difference in self-concept of both the groups was accepted. The study of Nayal et al. (1988) seems to contradict the finding of the present study in which science students were found to be significantly higher on self-concept than arts students.

Table 5.5: Comparison of Arts and Commerce Students on Self-concept

Sl. No.	*Measures of self-concept*	*Arts N = 200*		*Commerce N = 200*		*SED*	*t-value*
		Mean	*S.D.*	*Mean*	*S.D.*		
1.	Physical (A)	28.65	4.03	28.32	4.44	0.42	0.79
2.	Social (B)	28.75	4.35	29.79	4.57	0.44	2.36*
3.	Temperamental (C)	29.76	4.02	28.94	3.53	0.37	2.22*
4.	Educational (D)	32.52	4.25	26.56	5.32	0.48	12.42**
5.	Moral (E)	31.53	5.07	30.12	4.11	0.46	3.07**
6.	Intellectual (F)	27.06	3.95	25.23	5.04	0.46	3.98**
7.	Total	178.26	17.66	168.94	15.04	1.64	5.68**

* $p < .05$.

** $p < .01$.

It may be said on the basis of Table 5.5 that the structure and organization of the self-concepts of arts and commerce students are different from one another (cf., Fig. 4) on all the dimensions of self-concept (excepting physical self-concept, $t = 0.79$) there were significant differences between the mean scores of arts and commerce students. The mean scores of arts students were significantly higher on temperamental, educational, moral, intellectual and even on total self-concept. On the other hand, mean score of

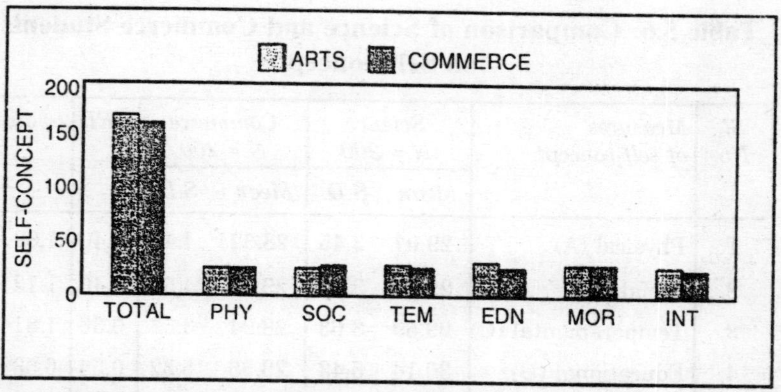

Fig. 4. Bar Diagram Showing Mean Scores of Self-concept for Arts and Commerce Students.

commerce students as compared to arts students was higher on social dimension of self-concept. This may mean that in comparison to commerce students, arts students perceive themselves to be more reactionary to a particular kind of emotion. Also, they perceive themselves in relation to school, teachers and extracurricular activities and they are aware of their intelligence and capacity of problem-solving and judgments. Further their estimation of their moral worth right and wrong activities is quite alarming. As a whole arts students exhibited better perception of themselves than their commerce counterparts. The commerce students yielded significantly higher score on the social scale than the arts students. In comparison to arts students, commerce students perceive themselves to be more sociable and thus view their sense of worth in social interactions. Hence the null hypothesis (i.e., 3b) was rejected excepting physical dimension of self-concept.

Table 5.6 shows that Science and Commerce students offered significantly with respect to two dimensions of self-concept, namely educational and moral, and also on total self-concept. Hence the null hypothesis (i.e., 3c) was rejected in case of two dimensions of self-concept (i.e., educational and moral) and also in case of total self-concept. The mean scores of science students were significantly higher on both

Table 5.6: Comparison of Science and Commerce Students on Self-concept

Sl. No.	*Measures of self-concept*	*Science N = 200*		*Commerce N = 200*		*SED*	*t-value*
		Mean	*S.D.*	*Mean*	*S.D.*		
1.	Physical (A)	29.07	3.45	28.32	4.44	0.40	1.88
2.	Social (B)	29.34	3.47	29.79	4.57	0.40	1.13
3.	Temperamental (C)	29.59	3.63	28.94	3.53	0.36	1.81
4.	Educational (D)	30.14	5.43	29.56	5.32	0.54	6.53**
5.	Moral (E)	31.82	3.93	30.12	4.11	0.40	4.25**
6.	Intellectual (F)	25.63	4.15	25.23	5.04	0.47	0.85
7.	Total	175.59	17.68	168.94	15.04	1.64	4.05**

** $p < .01$.

educational and moral measures of self-concept and also on total self-concept (cf., Fig. 5). This may mean that in comparison to commerce students, science students yielded significantly higher score on the educational, moral and total self-concept scales. It seems safe to interpret that science students as compared to commerce students perceive themselves in relation to school, teachers and extra-curricular activities and they also estimate their moral worth; right or

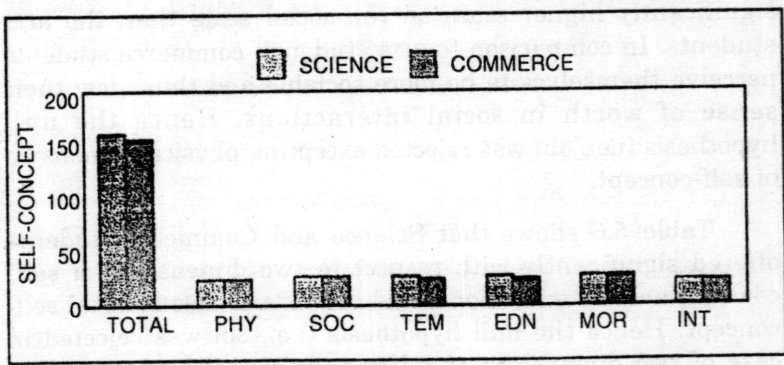

Fig. 5. Bar Diagram Showing Mean Scores of Self-concept for Science and Commerce Students.

wrong activities. They are more aware of themselves as a person as related to the world in which they live. Both the groups, however, occupied similar position in case of physical, social, temperamental and intellectual dimensions of self-concept. Hence, the results were partly in accordance with the conjecture (i.e., 3c).

LEVEL OF ACHIEVEMENT AND SELF-CONCEPT

The self-concept affects academic achievement (Sharma, 1983). The different areas of self-concept have significant bearing on academic achievement. Sharma (1983), for example reported that intellectual and school status has been conducive to high achievement on the other hand, the self-concept of physical appearance and attributes has inverse relationship with academic achievement. A large number of researches have been conducted to analyse the relationship between students self-concept and their achievement. It is found that high achievers in schools and colleges possess a feeling a adequacy. Very few studies have been conducted to compare the high and low achievers on self-concept. A comparative study of the organisation of self-concept in high and low achievers made by Sharma (1983) brought out the important areas of self-concept contributing to high achievement were intellectual and school status, and physical appearance and attributes. Here an attempt is made to compare the high and low achievers on their self-concept. It was hypothesized that there would be no significant difference in the self-concept of high and low achievers. In order to test this hypothesis comparisons were made between high and low achievers on self-concept. For the purpose the achievement scores of the sampled students were tabulated into frequency distribution and the distribution was normal. In order to compare the high and low achievers on their self-concept P_{75} and P_{25} were calculated respectively for identifying high and low achievers. The P_{75} and P_{25} values are 59 and 45 respectively. On the basis of this, it can be said that a student who scores 59 or more is a high achiever and a student who scores 45 or less is a low achiever. In this way a total of 144 high achievers and 142 low achievers were identified (cf., Appendix B_2 and B_3). Comparison between the high and low achievers was made on the basis of the '*t*' test with 0.05 and 0.01 levels of confidence for significance. The results are summarised in Table 5.7.

Table 5.7: Comparison of High Achievers and Low Achievers on Self-concept

Sl. No.	*Measures of self-concept*	*High achievers N = 200*		*Low achievers N = 200*		*SED*	*t-value*
		Mean	*S.D.*	*Mean*	*S.D.*		
1.	Physical (A)	29.03	4.40	29.22	3.76	0.48	0.40
2.	Social (B)	29.41	4.71	29.85	3.51	0.49	0.90
3.	Temperamental (C)	30.54	3.92	29.35	3.57	0.45	2.64**
4.	Educational (D)	33.78	3.15	27.66	6.22	0.58	10.55**
5.	Moral (E)	32.28	3.95	30.74	4.83	0.52	2.96**
6.	Intellectual (F)	29.33	4.22	24.69	4.52	0.51	9.10**
7.	Total	184.46	13.41	171.49	15.23	1.70	7.63**

** $p < .01$.

It may be said on the basis of Table 5.7 that the structure and organization of the self-concepts of high and low achievers were different from one other (cf., Fig. 6) on four out of six aspects of self-concept too and in total self-concept too, there were significant differences between the mean scores of high and low achievers. The mean scores of high and low achievers were significantly higher on all the four dimensions of self-concept (i.e., temperamental educational, moral intellectual) and even on total self-concept. This may mean that in comparison to low achievers, high achievers perceive themselves to be more emotionally stable. Also, they perceive themselves to be students who had more positive feelings towards school, teachers and extra-curricular activities. They also estimate their moral worth; right and wrong activities positively. They were quite aware. of their intelligence and capacity of problem-solving and judgments.

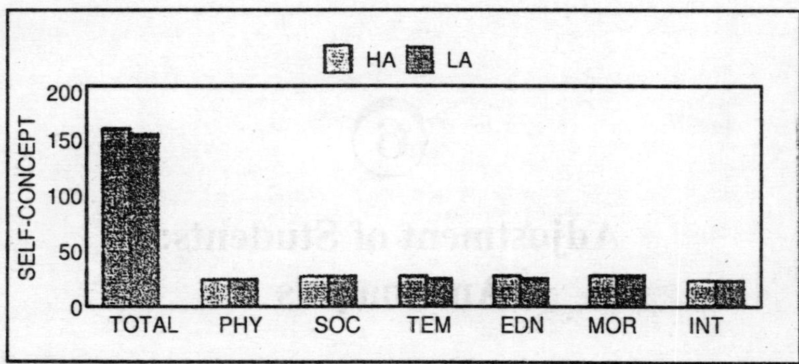

Fig. 6: Bar Diagram Showing Mean Scores of Self-concept for High and Low Achievers.

On the whole the high and low achievers differed significantly on their total self-concept. Bhatnagar (1970) observed that low achievement in case of students had its genesis in how they view themselves. Rao (1963) reported that over-achievers tend to differ significantly from both normal and under-achievers and that over-achievers have optimum adjustment to achievement situations. However, the high and low achievers did not differ significantly on rest of the self-concepts (i.e., physical and social). It implies that both the groups occupied the similar position in case of physical and social self-concepts. In view of the above results, the null hypotheses (i.e., H-7) was partly rejected and partly accepted.

Adjustment of Students: An Analysis

Personality of an individual consist of his persistent tendencies to make adjustment between his needs and environment. A balanced personality is the outcome of proper adjustment of an individual to his social environment. Psychologically adjustment may be seen as a process by means of which an individual makes an effort to establish equilibrium. Maladjustment leads to various personality complexities. Rao (1968) once remarked that a large section of the student community are feeling bewildered and have emotional and social problems of adjustment. Personal as well as social adjustment plays an important role in the academic achievement and the personality growth of the adolescents. Rohela (1969) has also mentioned that students who are undergoing a period of stress and strain, anxiety and tension are not able to adjust themselves to the life at school and outside it. In case of personal adjustment. Entiwistle and Cunningham (1968) have found that neuroticism showed a significant correlation with school attainment. Seidman (1955) reports that the academic progress of the child is affected by his emotions and feelings.

In this chapter an attempt has been made to analyze the adjustment pattern of sampled students across their sex, residential background, academic streams and levels of achievement.

TESTING THE NORMALCY OF DISTRIBUTION OF THE ADJUSTMENT SCORES

The second and fourth objectives of the investigation was

Table 6.1: Values of Skewness and Kurtosis of Adjustment (i.e., dimension-wise and total)

Sl. No.	*Variables*	*Male*		*Female*		*Urban*		*Rural*		*Science*		*Arts*		*Commerce*		*High achivers*		*Low achivers*	
		Sk	*Ku*	*Sk*	*Ku*	*Sk*	*Ku*	*Sk*	*Ku*	*Sk*	*Ku*	*Sk*	*Ku*	*Sk*	*Ku*	*Sk*	*Ku*	*Sk*	*Ku*
1.	Adjustment (Total)	0.21	0.18	–1.10	0.21	–0.91	0.02	0.18	0.11	0.07	0.09	0.00	0.15	0.16	0.05	0.17	0.04	0.20	0.14
2.	Emotional	0.17	0.07	0.13	0.07	–0.39	0.21	0.22	0.08	0.09	0.20	0.16	0.09	0.05	0.17	0.14	0.10	0.17	0.18
3.	Social	0.16	0.12	0.17	0.12	0.13	0.08	–1.23	0.18	0.01	0.11	–0.42	0.07	0.12	0.16	0.11	0.05	–0.30	0.21
4.	Educational	0.19	0.17	0.07	0.15	0.18	0.05	0.17	0.19	0.06	0.14	0.19	0.13	0.16	0.19	0.13	0.03	0.09	0.20

to study the adjustment pattern of the students across their sex, residential background and academic streams; and levels of achievement respectively. Data on adjustment from the selected subjects were obtained by administering Sinha and Singh's (1993) Adjustment Inventory. The distribution of scores on adjustment (i.e., dimension-wise and total) for the male, female, urban, rural, arts, science, commerce students together with high and low achievers were examined in respect of their nature and departure from normalcy. For the purpose indices of Skewness and Kurtosis were computed following the percentile method suggested by Garrett (1971). Table 6.1 shows the findings in this regard.

The values of Skewness and Kurtossi (Vide Table 6.1) for all the dependent variables, except a few ones, indicated near normality. In the light of the remarks made by Boneau (1960), it was decided to use *'t'* test for the above variable.

SEX AND ADJUSTMENT

Sex has been considered as an important factor in determining one's adjustment. There are empirical evidences (e.g., Asha, 1978; Sharma, 1979; Mattoo, 1980; Swain and Panda, 1982; Saraswat, 1986; Sunita, 1986; Sethy, 1993; Keshap, 1993; Chauhan and Murthy, 1994; Kasinath, 2000) which support sex differences in adjustment. On the other hand, the study of Parween (1958), Nominee (1965) has reported no sex difference in adjustment. In view of the above results an attempt is made here to find out the differences if any between the male and female students in their patterns of adjustment. Comparison of the above two groups was made on the basis of the *'t'*-test with 0.05 and 0.01 levels of confidence for significance. The relevant results are presented in Table 6.2.

Table 6.2 indicates that male and female students did not differ significantly in their total adjustment. It tends to mean that both male and female students occupied the similar position in their total adjustment. Therefore, the off-quoted belief that boys are better adjusted than the girls was shattered on the basis of the statistics shown in Table 6.2,

Table 6.2: Comparison of Male and Female Students on Adjustment

Sl. No.	*Adjustment Areas*	*Male students N = 300*		*Female students N = 300*		*SED*	*t-value*
		Mean	*S.D.*	*Mean*	*S.D.*		
1.	Emotional (A)	6.6	3.2	6.23	3.17	0.24	1.54
2.	Social (B)	6.39	3.9	5.46	2.99	0.24	3.88**
3.	Educational (C)	7.06	4.47	7.40	4.65	0.37	0.92
4.	Total	20.05	8.21	19.10	8.34	0.67	1.42

** $p < .01$.

thus it can be said that gender has no influence on the pattern of one's adjustment. So the null hypothesis was retained here. However, areawise analysis of adjustment shows sex difference in respect to social adjustment. It may be recalled that a higher scores on the adjustment inventory speaks of maladjustment or poor adjustment and vice-versa. Hence it can be said that female students appeared to have better social adjustment ability than their male counterparts. This may be due to the very setting of the present era. These days sex discrimination in relation to the status has been minimized. The age-old dominance of man over women has been ruled out. The girls enjoy no less status in social, economic and political life. The modern way of living has made the female students to be cooperative, friendly. They enjoy working together, actively participate in school/college assemblies, never hesitate to get ideas from others and like to work together. Here the null hypotheses was rejected. As regards the emotional and educational adjustment, the differences were not significant. It implies that both male and female students have similar inclination towards emotional maturity and behaviour and educational growth. Here the null hypothesis was retained.

Figure 1 presents a comparative picture of adjustment of male and female students.

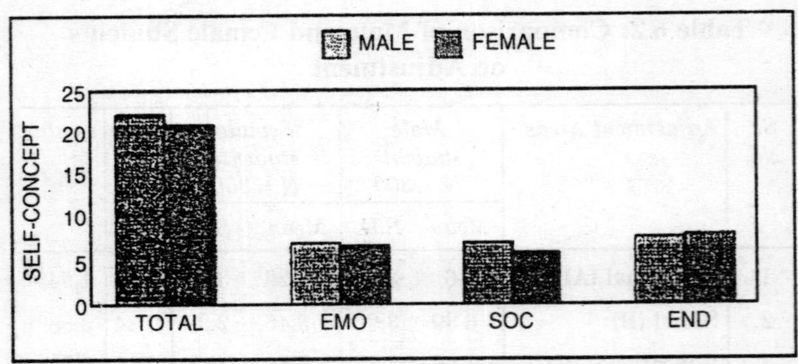

Fig. 1: Bar Diagram Showing Mean Scores of Adjustment for Male and Female Students.

RESIDENTIAL BACKGROUND AND ADJUSTMENT

In pursuance of the objective (i.e., 2.3.2) of the investigation, "to study the adjustment patterns of students having rural-urban background" significance of difference between relevant means were tested by employing '*t*' test. The obtained results have been presented in Table 6.3.

Table 6.3: Comparison of Urban and Rural Students on Adjustment

Sl. No.	*Adjustment Areas*	*Urban N = 300*		*Rural N = 300*		*SED*	*t-value*
		Mean	*S.D.*	*Mean*	*S.D.*		
1.	Emotional (A)	6.30	3.2	6.54	3.18	0.24	1.00
2.	Social (B)	5.97	3.11	5.88	2.84	0.24	0.38
3.	Educational (C)	6.46	4.14	8.01	4.82	0.37	4.19**
4.	Total	18.73	8.26	20.42	8.22	0.68	2.49*

*$p < .05$.

**$p < .01$.

Table 6.3 indicates that the *t*-value (i.e., 4.19) between urban and rural students in educational area of adjustment was significant even at .01 level. It means that the students from rural areas differed significantly from their urban counterparts in respect to educational adjustment and the difference was in favour of urban students (i.e., low score indicates better adjustment). It may be interpreted that students hailing from rural areas have greater adjustment problems than urban students in educational area. This may be due to family background and differences in their socio-cultural settings. The present finding is substantiated by the finding of the study conducted by Singh and Singh (1987) who found that rural students were less adjusted on emotional and educational adjustment than the urban students. Similar was the finding in case of total adjustment. The students hailing from urban areas were found to have better adjustment than their rural counterparts. Such a situation may be attributed to their family back ground. Most of the urban students belong to high socio-economic status families. Their socio-cultural settings are varied and conductive for better social interaction and educational provisions. They are more explicitly expected by their parents to keep pace with educational growth norms. It is natural that they are much more concerned with these adjustment patterns. The result support the findings of Pandey (1979) and Tripathi (1981) who found residential differences in adjustment.

Graphical representation of data was also attempted in Figure 2 which shows variance in the adjustment for urban and rural students.

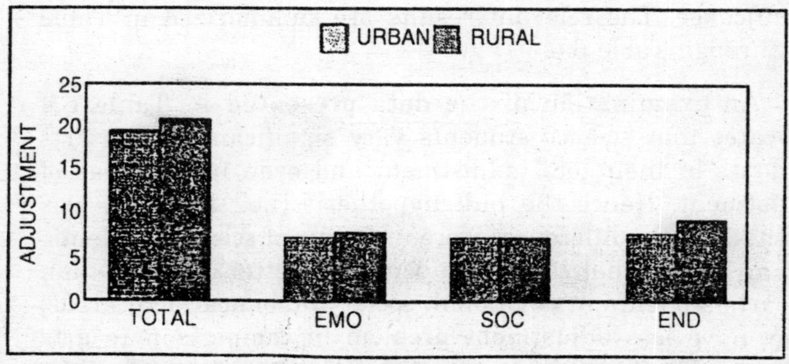

Fig. 2: Bar Diagram Showing Mean Scores of Adjustment for Urban and Rural Students.

However, rural and urban students did not differ significantly in respect to emotional and social adjustment. Hence, the null hypothesis was retained showing thereby the similar inclination towards emotional and social adjustment. In view of the above results, the null hypothesis (i.e., H-5) stands partly accepted and partly rejected.

ACADEMIC STREAM AND ADJUSTMENT

An attempt has been made here to compare the adjustment patterns of students belonging to three different academic streams, namely science, arts and commerce. It was hypothesized that there would be no significant difference in the adjustment (i.e., area-wise and total) of: (a) arts and science students; (b) arts and commerce students; and (c) science and commerce students.

In order to test this hypothesis, comparisons were made between arts and science students, between arts and commerce students, and between science and commerce students on adjustment as measured by Sinha and Singh (1993). The scores obtained by arts, science and commerce students on three areas of adjustment namely, emotional, social and educational and total too were tabulated separately into frequency distributions. Mean scores and SDs for each group on three scales and total scale were calculated comparisons among the groups were made on the basis of the '*t*'-test with 0.05 level on 0.01 level of confidence for significance. The relevant results are summarized in Table 6.4 through Table 6.6.

An examination of the data presented in Table 6.4 indicates that science students vary significantly from arts students in their total adjustment and even in all areas of adjustment. Hence the null hypothesis [i.e., H-6 (a)], was rejected. These differences were in favour of science students. It may be said that science students are better adjusted than the arts students in emotional, social and educational areas. They have less adjustment problem in comparison to arts students. This may be due to the following facts. That the students who entered into the science stream remained busy

Table 6.4: Comparison of Arts and Science Students on Adjustment

Sl. No.	*Adjustment Areas*	*Arts N = 200*		*Science N = 200*		*SED*	*t-value*
		Mean	*S.D.*	*Mean*	*S.D.*		
1.	Emotional (A)	6.77	3.05	5.73	3.28	0.32	3.25**
2.	Social (B)	6.65	2.4	5.30	3.34	0.30	4.50**
3.	Educational (C)	7.24	3.35	6.23	5.21	0.45	2.24*
4.	Total	20.65	6.21	17.25	9.69	0.81	4.20**

*p < .05.

**p < .01.

in their academic pursuits. In comparison to the arts students, science students are academically sound and they have high educational aspiration. For this they pay attention study, interact with the teachers, parents and friends. They take the advantages of social setting for their academic pursuits. This may result some kind of satisfaction in them and may lead to emotional stability. Kumar, Singh and Mohammed (1995) also concluded that science students were better adjusted than the arts students in all dimensions. However Sharma (1986) reported that arts students had more problems than the

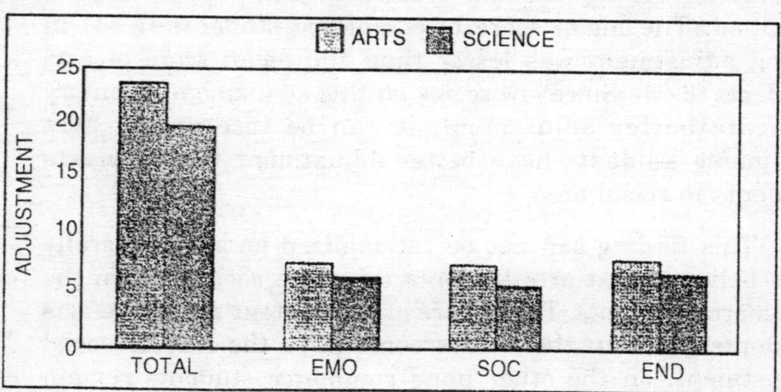

Fig. 3: Bar Diagram Showing Mean Scores of Adjustment for Arts and Science Students.

science students in home and health areas. But the present finding contradicts the finding of Agarwal and Sonawat (1991) who found that arts students in comparison to science students were better adjusted in emotional area.

Figure 3 presents a comparative picture of adjustment of arts and science students.

Table 6.5: Comparison of Arts and Commerce Students on Adjustment

Sl. No.	*Adjustment Areas*	*Arts N = 200*		*Commerce N = 200*		*SED*	*t-value*
		Mean	*S.D.*	*Mean*	*S.D.*		
1.	Emotional (A)	6.77	3.05	6.76	3.13	0.32	0.03
2.	Social (B)	6.65	2.4	5.84	2.97	0.26	3.12**
3.	Educational (C)	7.24	3.35	8.24	4.69	0.41	2.44*
4.	Total	20.65	6.21	20.83	8.09	0.72	0.25

* $p < .05$.

** $p < .01$.

Table 6.5 indicates that the *t*-values (3.12 and 2.44) between arts and commerce students in social and educational areas of adjustment were significant at 0.01 and 0.05 level respectively. Hence the null hypothesis [i.e., H-6 (b)] was not retained. The mean score of commerce students (5.84) in social adjustment was lesser than the mean score of arts students (6.65). Since low scores on this adjustment inventory indicate better adjustment, it can be interpreted that commerce students have better adjustment than the arts students in social area.

This finding can not be rationalized because generally it is believed that arts students are more sociable than the commerce students. The nature of the content which the arts students learn in their classrooms pave the way of social adjustment, on the other hand commerce students remain busy in their studies. The content of commerce hardly gives the scope to mix with others, to do things cooperatively. The present finding contradicts the finding of Agarwal and Sonawat (1991).

On the other hand, arts students have better adjustment as compared to the commerce students in educational area. This may be due to their higher level of involvement in studies. In order to achieve academic excellence, the arts students like to think more for their studies, examination etc., to be confident in their learning, they consult their teachers, attend classes regularly, discuss academic issues with their class-fellows. They learn the material in order to perform better. For getting the good grades they compete with others. They take part in as much as of the class-related activities as possible and little that is not the part of course outline. All these lead to their better adjustment in educational area. No parallel study is made available to support or contradict the present finding.

However, in emotional area of adjustment and total adjustment, arts and commerce students were found to be alike. This finding contradicts the finding of Agarwal and Sonawat (1991) who reported that arts students were better adjusted than the commerce students in emotional area.

Figure 4 displays variance in the adjustment patterns of students belonging to arts and commerce streams.

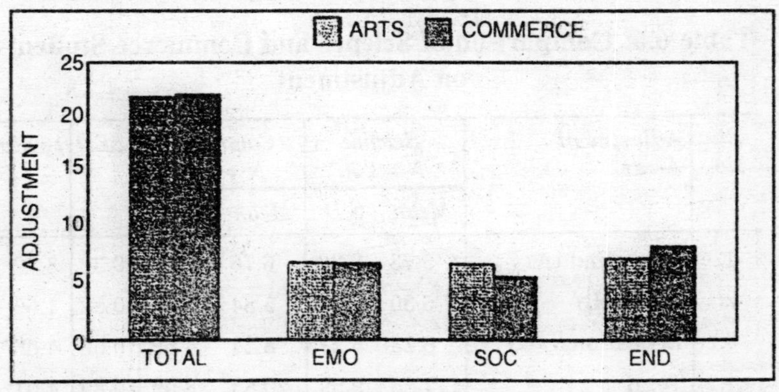

Fig. 4: Bar Diagram Showing Mean Scores of Adjustment for Arts and Commerce Students.

It is evident from Table 6.6 that significant differences existed in mean scores of science and commerce students with respected to their emotional ($t = 3.22, p < .01$), educational ($t = 4.06, p < .01$) and total ($t = 4.01, p < .01$) adjustment. The mean scores of commerce students as compared to science students are significantly higher in emotional, educational and total adjustment. This may mean that in comparison to science students, commerce students have greater adjustment problems in emotional and educational areas and even in total adjustment. Such finding may be justified in view of the nature of the content which the science students learn in their class room. The content of science is relatively more difficult and require more attention of the students while they learn than their counterparts commerce students. The science students to feel confident in their learning abilities remain busy in studies. To compete with others in the class for getting the rewards they cooperate more with teachers and peers and like more to work with others. They take the responsibility for getting the most out of the class and participate with others when to do so, they try to learn the most by sharing ideas and talents.

The obtained findings do not get direct support from any study because on Indian population there seems to be no research precedence, particularly related to differences in

Table 6.6: Comparison of Science and Commerce Students on Adjustment

Sl. No.	*Adjustment Areas*	*Science N = 200*		*Commerce N = 200*		*SED*	*t-value*
		Mean	*S.D.*	*Mean*	*S.D.*		
1.	Emotional (A)	5.73	3.28	6.76	3.13	0.32	3.22**
2.	Social (B)	5.30	3.34	5.84	2.97	0.32	1.69
3.	Educational (C)	6.23	5.21	8.24	4.69	0.50	4.06**
4.	Total	17.25	9.69	20.83	8.09	0.89	4.01**

** $p < .01$.

adjustment patterns of science and commerce students by using adjustment inventory of Sinha and Singh (1993). Some studies, however, employing different tools of adjustment have shown differences in adjustment of students belonging to different academic streams (Sharma, 1986; Agarwal and Sonawat, 1991; Kumar, Singh and Mohammed, 1995).

However, both the groups (i.e., science vs. commerce) were found to be similar with regards to their social adjustment.

In view of the above results, the null hypothesis [i.e., 6-(C)] was partly accepted and partly rejected.

Figure 5 gives a comparative picture of adjustment of science and commerce students.

LEVEL OF ACHIEVEMENT AND ADJUSTMENT

Adjustment is a core mental health dimension and good adjustment leads to improved academic achievement (Rao, 1972; Kohli, 1975; Narang, 1981; Gulati, 1982; Mohan and

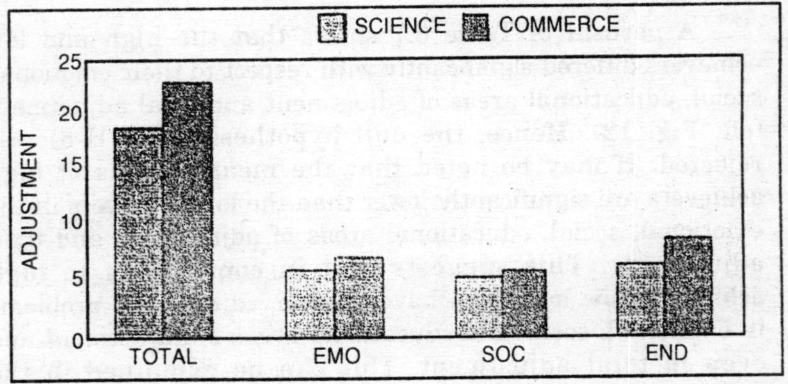

Fig. 5: Bar Diagram Showing Mean Scores of Adjustment for Science and Commerce Students.

Gulati, 1983; Royer, 1984 and Sharma 1983), however, did not find adjustment to be a significant contributor to achievement. Rao (1963) reported that the over-achievers tend to differ significantly from both normal-achievers and under-achievers and that the over-achiever has the optimum adjustment to achievement situations. Tripathi (1966) reported that low and under-achieving students reveal a significantly greater number of problems that high achieving college students. Sinha (1966) found a clear-cut distinction between high and low achievers on anxiety and general adjustment inventory. Vishnoi (1974) found high achievers to be better adjusted than low achievers in the five areas of adjustment as well as the total adjustment scores. On the other hand, Sharma (1983) did not find significant difference between high and low achievers on adjustment scores. In view of the contradictory results, an attempt is made here to compare the high and low achievers with respect to their adjustment. It was hypothesized that there would be no significant difference between the high and low achievers in their adjustment (area-wise and total). In order to test this hypothesis comparisons were made between the high and low achievers in their adjustment. Comparison between the high and low achievers was made on the basis of the '*t*'-test with 0.05 and 0.01 levels of confidence for significance. The results are presented in Table 6.7.

A perusal of Table 6.7 shows that the high and low achievers differed significantly with respect to their emotional, social, educational areas of adjustment and total adjustment (cf., Fig. 12). Hence, the null hypothesis (i.e., H-8) was rejected. If may be noted that the means scores of high achievers are significantly lower than the low achievers in the emotional, social, educational areas of adjustment and total adjustment. This suggests that in comparison to high achievers, low achievers have greater adjustment problems in emotional, social and educational areas of adjustment and even in total adjustment. This can be explained in the following way. It is generally believed that a student's academic achievement is a function of his response sets and learning experiences determined by his personality factors, adjustment, motivation, goals etc. Considering that a students performance is a part function of his whole personality, his adjustment, etc., the part played by these non-intellectual factors in achievement appears to assume greater importance

Table 6.7: Comparison of High and Low Achievers on Adjustment

Sl. No.	*Adjustment Areas*	*High achievers N = 144*		*Low achievers N = 142*		*SED*	*t-value*
		Mean	*S.D.*	*Mean*	*S.D.*		
1.	Emotional (A)	3.99	1.94	7.89	2.94	0.30	13.00**
2.	Social (B)	3.67	2.23	7.33	2.14	0.24	15.25**
3.	Educational (C)	2.30	1.45	11.13	3.79	0.33	26.76**
4.	Total	9.95	4.13	26.36	6.3	0.63	26.05**

** $p < .01$.

at higher levels of education. Superior achievement may be thus, related to successful adjustment. That a student fails to make the grades he is capable of might have for its explanation some upset or undesirable mode of adjustment to the demands of the new environment into which he enters after school.

Students resort to colleges from no common motives and carry dispositions favourable or hostile to satisfactory adjustment. Some are keen and adequately motivated, they are avid of learning and develop sound techniques for

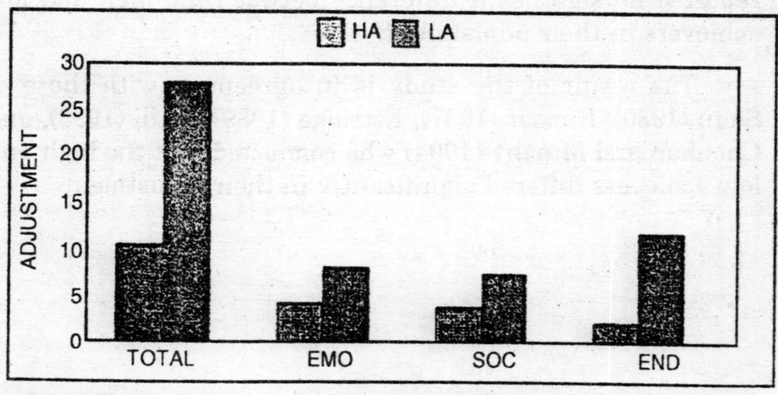

Fig. 6: Bar Diagram Showing Mean Scores of Adjustment for High and Low Achievers.

acquiring it. They adjust reasonably well to their class-fellows and teachers. Others fare less fortunately. Some become home-sick while a few get themselves wrapped up in difficulties, grow listless, seek various forms of retreat, like wandering, day, dreaming etc. Some try and succeed getting the attention of their fellow and conduct themselves as if they resort to colleges in order to be noticed, to be hoisted into the status of leadership and to be admired. Still others just drift along, letting themselves to be pushed and pulled by adventitious forces. Thus the adjustment process and their perversions adopted by students may perhaps hold the key to understanding of the phenomenon of under-achievement. Stenizor (1944), Cattell (1945), Thompson (1948) pointed out that the over-achievers were characterized by good adjustment to school and greater awareness and responsiveness to environmental influences. Johnson (1947) held that poor performance in college was due to unsatisfactory adjustment to college. According to Anderson (1954) many under-achievers were not beset with serious personal problems. Their difficulty seems to lie in an inadequate understanding of the academic challenge coupled with an equally inadequate effort.

However, some other researchers like Swain and Panda (1982), Sharma (1983), Kaile and Kaur (1995) and Nair (1999) reported no significant difference between the high and low achievers in their adjustment.

The result of the study is in agreement with those of Saun (1980), Kapoor (1987), Estridge (1989), Sethi (1993), and Chouhan and Murthy (1994) who conducted that the high and low achievers differed significantly in their adjustment.

Interrelationship among the Variables

The present Chapter deals with the relationship among self-concept, adjustment and academic achievement of students. Therefore, a discussion of the relationship between the following pairs of variables selected for the study of students is presented:

1. Self-concept and Academic Achievement,
2. Adjustment and Academic Achievement, and
3. Self-concept and Adjustment

To ascertain the relationship among the selected variables in different pairs of combinations, Pearson's product moment coefficients of correlation's were calculated.

It may be stated again that in the present study the low scores on the adjustment inventory indicate a better adjustment, whereas the higher scores on it are indicative of a poor adjustment. The implication of the scoring of this type is that in such cases, the negative *'r'* value is to be interpreted as a positive relationship. Wherever such a situation obtained, it has been stated so at the time of discussion of such relationship. On the other hand the scores on the self-concept questionnaire are to be interpreted in usual manner.

RELATIONSHIP BETWEEN SELF-CONCEPT AND ACADEMIC ACHIEVEMENT

Recently, there has been a growing tendency to emphasize the non-intellectual and dynamic factors in the student's performance (Garrett, 1949; Beasley, 1957). A wide variety of personality traits have been hypothesized as factors of academic achievement. McCandles (1961) predicted that "poor self-concepts, implying as they often do a lack of confidence in facing and mastering the environment, might accompany deficiency in one of the most vital of the child's areas of accomplishment—his performance in school".

Several studies have been conducted to find out the relationship between the self-concept and school achievement. In a study by Coppersmith (1959), a correlation of 0.36 was found between positive self-concept and school achievement. Jayaswal (1973) studied the relationship between self-concept and school marks and found it to be positive but negligible. Bhatnagar (1970) found that low achievement in case of students had its genesis in how they view themselves. On the other hand Deo and Bhullar (1974), and Sharma (1983) found no relationship between self-concept and achievement. All these studies are not in agreement with one another. Therefore, the researcher has made an attempt to find out the relationship between self-concept and achievement.

In this connection it was hypothesized that there would be no significant relationship between self-concept (dimension-wise and total and academic achievement). The relationship between these two variables was computed by employing Pearsons' product moment correlation and the results are presented in Table 7.1.

It may be observed from Table 7.1 that the coefficients of correlation's between dimensions of self-concept and academic achievement ranged from –0.02 to 0.43. All these coefficients of correlation's except for physical and social dimensions of self-concept are positive and significant. So it can be said that there exists significant relationship between the various dimensions of self-concept (i.e., temperamental, educational, moral, intellectual and total) achievement and the finding do not lend support to the hypothesis that there would be no significant relationship between self-concept (dimension-wise and total) and academic achievement (except physical and social dimensions).

Table 7.1: Coefficients of Correlation of Various Dimensions of Self-concept with Academic Achievement (N = 600)

Dimensions of self-concept	*Academic Achievement*
Total self-concept	0.34**
Physical (A)	–0.03
Social (B)	–0.02
Temperamental (C)	0.15**
Educational (D)	0.43**
Moral (E)	0.15**
Intellectual (F)	0.38**

** $p < .01$.

The results suggested that the self-concept affects academic achievement. The four areas of self-concept which have significant bearing on academic achievement are temperamental, educational, moral and intellectual. It can safety be interpreted that a student who perceives himself in relation to school, teachers and extracurricular activities with predominance of a particular kind of emotional reaction and estimation of his moral worth and his awareness of his intelligence and capacity of problem-solving and judgments is expected to achieve more. This may be the reason why achievement is associated positively with self-concept. The findings of this study are corroborated by the findings of Morgan (1952), Holland and Astin (1962), Bhatnagar (1970), Bittner (1971), Jayaswal (1973), Saraswat (1982), Sharma (1983), Singh (1987), Barry (1991) and Shah (1998) who found that self-concept has a bearing on academic achievement. But there are other studies that contradict the results of the present study. In their studies Carey (1977) Saunders (1978) and Maikhuri and Panda (1971) found that there was no correlation between self-concept and achievement. Spirack (1956) found that there was zero correlation between students' academic achievement and self-acceptance. Bruce and Howard (1977) reported that high school students' achievement was no related to their self-concept.

RELATIONSHIP BETWEEN ADJUSTMENT AND ACADEMIC ACHIEVEMENT

Adjustment is a continual process by which a person varies his behaviour to produce a more harmonious relationship between himself and his environment. The direction of his effort may be towards modifying his own behaviour and attitude towards changing the environment or both.

Several investigations have found the area of adjustment to college to be of vital importance in academic achievement. As early as 1927, Corson (1927), observed that on entering the college, the Freshman faces a number of new adjustment problems for which he is usually unprepared, Congdon (1943), Houston and Marzolf (1944), Hibler and Larson (1944), Carroll and Jones (1944), Agarwal (1960), Kakkar (1964), Badami (1973), Srinivasan (1974), Swain and Panda (1982) have all found several adjustment problems to be associated with under-achievement. Stone (1948) located problems in the area of adjustment to college work and found then to rank first in a study of 578 students.

From the Welter of these findings one can discern a factor which may be identified as "adjustment to academic work", that is either directly or indirectly found to be operative in precipitating under-achievement in the academic scene. If adjustment affects academic achievement then to what extent and in what direction? Therefore, the relationship between adjustment and academic achievement has been studied on a representative sample of 600 students.

It was hypothesized that there would be no significant relationship between adjustment (area-wise and total) and academic achievement. The relationship between these two variables was computed by employing Pearson's product moment correlation and the results are given in Table 7.2.

All the coefficients of correlation (vide Table 7.2) were obtained in negative which, in fact, show a positive relationship since higher scores on the adjustment inventory

Table 7.2: Coefficient of Correlation of Different Areas of Adjustment with Academic Achievement (N = 600)

Areas of adjustment	*Academic achievement*
Total Adjustment	-0.75**
Emotional	-0.53**
Social	-0.49**
Educational	-0.77**

** $p < .01$.

speak of a greater maladjustment and vice-versa. The coefficient of correlation ranged from 0.49 (Social adjustment) to 0.77 (educational adjustment) which are significant at 0.01 level. So there exists a significant relationship between adjustment (area-wise and total) and academic achievement. This indicates that the two variables are significantly related with each other. It perhaps shows that if the adjustment of students increases, achievement becomes higher and vice-versa. In other words, it can be said that better is the adjustment, more will be the achievement. Hence the null hypothesis that there will be no significant relationship between adjustment (areas-wise and total) and academic achievement was rejected.

This finding is not contrary to the general expectation and seems reasonable. Academic achievement, it would be appreciated, is the resultant of the complex patterns of adjustment which determine the efficiency of the individual's patterns of energy utilization. The pattern of adjustment to the academic situation, determines to a large extent the quality and efficiency of academic striving. Thus superior achievement may be looked upon as evidence of successful adjustment as it is the end product of the interplay of a complexity of factors specifically involved in the academic situation. The capacity to meet all the demands in the academic situation or some of them reasonably. Well, involves aspects of personality, like motivation, aspirations, goals, interests, study skills and practices, personal, social and emotional adjustment etc. Stormworld and Wrenn (1948) remarked that a well adjusted student exhibits high intrinsic interest in the subject-matter of study, positive attitude towards the requirements of his curriculum, stability of his goals, balanced emotional life, ability to concentrate for a reasonable length of time on his tasks and ability to enjoy life in many areas. Findings of Termini and Odeon (1947), Shaw and McCuen (1960), Gallenghar (1964) have emphasized that under-achievement is a continuing problem stemming from basic personality and social problems which needs treatment and care as early as in the school programme as is feasible. The present finding supports the findings of Rao (1971), Sharma (1983) and Rongali (1993) who found that academic achievement, was significantly related to students' adjustment. On the other hand, it contradicts the finding of Vishnoi (1947) who found no substantial relationship between personality adjustment and academic achievement.

RELATIONSHIP BETWEEN SELF-CONCEPT AND ADJUSTMENT

The studies in the area of self-concept as related to adjustment are quite few. William and Code (1968) studied self-concept and school adjustment and found a significant effect of self-concept on school adjustment. He reported that children having good self-concept adjust themselves in school easily in comparison to those having poor self-concept. Pathak (1966) found a positive relationship between the self-ideal congruence and adjustment. Sharma (1983) reported that low self-concept group was poor in adjustment as compared with the high self-concept groups. No study has tried to find out area-wise relationship between the two.

Therefore, here an attempt is made to find out the relationship between self-concept (dimension-wise and total), adjustment (area-wise and total). The null hypothesis maintains that there will be no significant relationship between self-concept (dimension-wise and total) and adjustment (area-wise and total). The relationship between these two variables has been computed by employing Pearson's Product Moment correlation and the results have been presented in Table 7.3.

Table 7.3: Co-efficient of Correlation of Different Dimensions of Self-concept with Various Areas of Adjustment (N = 600)

Adjustment / Self-concept	*Emotional*	*Social*	*Educational*	*Total*
Physical (A)	0.05	0.09*	0.01	0.05
Social (B)	–0.04	–0.27**	0.005	–0.10*
Temperamental (C)	–0.19**	–0.16**	–0.25**	–0.25**
Educational (D)	–0.41**	–0.19**	–0.60**	–0.52**
Moral (E)	–0.25**	–0.12**	–0.27**	–0.27**
Intellectual (F)	–0.29**	–0.14**	–0.46**	–0.39**
Total	–0.35**	–0.23**	–0.49**	–0.46**

*$p < .05$.

**$p < .01$.

It may be seen from Table 7.3 that the coefficients of correlation between dimensions of self-concept and areas of adjustment ranged from 0.005 to –0.60. It may be recalled that a higher score on the adjustment inventory speaks of maladjustment or poor adjustment. Hence, the obtained negative correlation is really indicative of a positive relationship and not a negative one. All the coefficients of correlation (except for physical self-concept and emotional adjustment; social self-concept and emotional adjustment, physical self-concept and educational adjustment; social self-concept and educational adjustment; physical self-concept and total adjustment) are positive and significant. So there is significant positive relationship between self-concept and adjustment. The different dimensions of self-concept, namely temperamental, educational, moral and intellectual affect the emotional adjustment of students. Similarly a student's social adjustment is being affected by his/her physical, social, temperamental, educational, moral and intellectual dimensions of self-concept and even by the total self-concept. The temperamental, educational, moral, intellectual dimensions of self-concept and total self-concept too have their bearing on the student's educational adjustment. On the other hand, the physical and social dimensions of self-concept do not affect one's emotional, educational and total adjustment. So it can be said that a student's emotional, educational and even total adjustment are independent of his/her physical and social self-concepts. These two dimensions of self-concept have nothing to do with one's emotional and educational adjustment and even with total adjustment.

Results reported above throw light on the interdependence of emotional adjustment and various dimensions of self-concept namely, temperamental, educational, moral, intellectual and total. It seems reasonable to state that if students perceive predominance of a particular kind of emotional reaction together with the view of themselves in relation to school, teachers and extracurricular activities and estimate their moral worth, being aware of their intelligence and capacity of problem-solving and judgements, could be emotionally stable. It could be so because most of the students perceive to release their pent up desires through their engagement in different curricular and co-curricular activities.

Similarly, social adjustment appears to be related with all dimensions of self-concept and even with total self-concept. It suggests that the students who tend to perceive themselves in terms of their body, health, physicial appearance and strength, in terms of their sense of worth in social interactions, in terms of their particular kind of emotional state, in terms of their relation to school, teachers and extra-curricular activities, in terms of estimation of their moral worth and in terms of their intelligence and capacity of problem solving and judgement are likely to have better social adjustment. Hence, the self-concept and social adjustment seem to move in the same direction.

Further, the significant relationship of different dimensions of self-concept with educational adjustment suggests that the students who tend to perceive themselves in terms of their prevailing emotional state, in terms of their relation to school, teachers and extra-curricular activities, in terms of estimation of their moral worth and in terms of their intelligence etc., are likely to have better educational adjustment. It is safe to say that the self-concept and educational adjustment seems to move in the same direction.

Similar was the result in case of the relationship between total self-concept and total adjustment. The findings indicates that the students who have superior self-concept are likely to be better adjusted and vice-versa. The finding is not contrary to a general expectation as the adjustment of a student is likely to be determined to an appreciable extent by his/her self-concept. As a matter of fact, the development of a healthy personality is largely determined by the way in which the adolescent is able to make adjustments in his life. A growing child has to successfully effect adjustment in various aspect of his life, like home, health, emotional, educational, social, personal, and son on. The extent and the mode of students' adjustment depends on their total collection of attitudes, judgements and values which they hold with respect to their behaviour, ability, body, worth as persons—in short how they perceive and evaluate themselves. Effective coping behaviour demands the sum of perceptions individuals hold about themselves as individuals and the way they relate to others and to the environment. This may be the reason why self-concept is associated positively with adjustment. No parallel study is available to support or contradict the findings of the study. However, the study of Pathak (1966) reported a positive relationship between the self-ideal congruence and adjustment. The null hypothesis for relationships of the two variables was, therefore, partially rejected.

Summary and Conclusion

CONTEXT OF THE STUDY

The fact of differences in school achievement, and the search for an explanation of those differences, is one of the most complex and at the present time, one of the most controversial issues in education today. It has been the focus of numerous researches and the topic of many government reports, not only in this country, but in most of the industrialized and industrializing countries of the world. Yet in spite of an impressive bibliography we are still almost as far from reaching an understating of the actual process of school achievement as we were some decades ago.

This is not to suggest that research has been altogether inconclusive. Although a detailed review of findings would be out of place here, such factors as parents, socio-economic status, family size, aspirations of both parents and children, and characteristics of the child such as ability, motivation and some personality traits have all been shown to be associated with school achievement in a wide variety of contexts. Moreover, in recent years a number of studies have attempted to assess the relative importance of these and other factors. For example, the Plowden Report, England (1967) attempted to differentiate the effect of home circumstances, including the physical amenities, the number of dependent children and parents' education, from the effect of parental attitudes and from the effect of the school. Similarly Coleman (1966) in a study undertaken on behalf of the US Office of Education, looked at the relative contribution of a number of aspects of the school.

There has been a growing tendency to emphasize the non-intellectual and dynamic factors in the student's performance (Beasley, 1957; Garrett, 1949). The investigations so far undertaken have tended to focus upon a wide variety of personality traits hypothesized as factors of academic achievement. McCandless (1961) predicted that 'poor self-concepts, implying as they often do a lack of confidence in facing and mastering the environment, might accompany deficiency in one of the most vital of the child's areas of accomplishment—his performance in school. Sinha (1966) reported that "as regards their self-concept, the low achievers tended to perceive themselves in a more favourable light".

Several investigators have found the area of adjustment to college to be of vital importance in academic achievement. As early as 1927, Corson (1927) observed that on entering the college, the freshman faces a number of new adjust mental problems for which he is usually unprepared. Congdon (1943), Houston and Marzolf (1944), Hibler and Larson (1944), Carroll and Jones (1944) have all found several adjustmental problems to be associated with under-achievement Steinzor (1944), Cattell (1945). Thompson (1948) also pointed out that the over-achievers were characterized by good adjustment to school and greater awareness and responsiveness to environmental influences. Johnson (1947) held that poor performance in college was due to unsatisfactory adjustment to college. Stormwold and Wrenn (1948) observed that a well-adjusted students exhibits high intrinsic interest in the subject matter of study, positive attitude towards the requirements of his curriculum, stability of his goals, balanced emotional life, ability to concentrate for reasonable length of time on his tasks, and ability to enjoy life in many areas. According to Anderson (1954) many under-achievers were not beset with serious personal problems. Their difficulty seems to lie in an inadequate understanding of the academic challenge coupled with an equally inadequate effort. Horrall (1957) studying students with high intelligence found that those adjudged to have good adjustment tended to be high achievers while those adjudged poorly adjusted to be low achievers. Findings of Terman and Oden (1947), Shaw and

McCuen (1960) and Gallenghar (1964) have emphasized that under-achievement is a continuing problem stemming from basic personality and social problems which needs treatment and care as early in the school programmes as is possible. French (1958) reported that lack of adjustment to college life in the freshman introduces extraneous influences on scholastic success, Christensen (1956) and Pophan and Moore (1960) observed that over-achievers significantly differ from under-achievers with regard to their adjustment to college as assessed by Borow's Inventory. Frankel (1960) found over-achievers to be more adequately adjusted to the academic situation. Rao (1967) found academic adjustment to be the greatest single factor that affected student performance. The present study aims at ascertaining the extent of influence of self-concept and adjustment on academic achievement.

OBJECTIVES

The objectives of the present study are:

1. To study the self concept of the students in relation to sex, place of residence (i.e., rural-urban), and academic streams (i.e., arts, science and commerce)
2. To study the adjustment of the students in relation to sex, place of residence and academic streams.
3. To compare the self-concept of high and low achievers.
4. To compare the adjustment pattern for high and low achievers.
5. To find out the relationship between self-concept (dimension-wise and total) and academic achievement.
6. To find out the relationship between adjustment (area-wise and total) and academic achievement.
7. To find out the relationship between self-concept (i.e., dimension wise and total) and adjustment (area-wise and total).

HYPOTHESES

In pursuance of the objectives of the study stated above, hypotheses were formulated and stated in the null form so that they could be tested statistically.

1. There is no significant sex difference in the self-concept (i.e., dimension-wise and total) of the students.
2. There is no significance difference in the self-concept (dimension-wise and total) or urban and rural students.
3. There is no significant difference in the self-concept (i.e., dimension-wise and total) of
   (a) Arts and science students,
   (b) Arts and commerce students, and
   (c) Science and commerce students.
4. There is no significant sex difference in the adjustment (i.e., area-wise and total) of the students.
5. There exists no significant difference in the adjustment (i.e., area-wise and total) of urban and rural students.
6. There is no significant difference in the adjustment (i.e., area-wise and total) of:
   (a) Arts and science students.
   (b) Arts and commerce students, and
   (c) Science and commerce students.
7. There is no significant difference between the high and low achievers in their self-concept (dimension-wise and total).
8. There is no significant difference between the high and low achievers in their adjustment (area-wise and total).

9. There will be no significant relationship between self-concept (dimension wise and total) and academic achievement of the students.

10. There will be no significant relationship between adjustment (area-wise and total) and academic achievement of the students.

11. There will be no significant relationship between self-concept (dimension-wise and total) and adjustment (area-wise and total) of the students.

COLLECTION OF DATA AND ITS TREATMENT

The subjects of the study were the higher secondary students studying in first year. Relevant data were collected from 600 students with the help of the following tools:

1. Self-concept Questionnaire by Saraswat (1984),

2. Adjustment Inventory by Sinha and Singh (1993).

However, no specific test was used to measure achievement. The total marks secured by the sample students in the Annual H.S.C. Examination, 1999 conducted by B.S.E., Orissa has been considered. Scoring procedure suggested by the test authors have been followed and after scoring the answer-sheets, the statistical treatment given to data included the *'t'* test and product moment correlation.

MAJOR FINDINGS

The preceding three chapters have been devoted to the analyses and interpretations of data. The analyses have yielded some significant findings pertaining to the students' self-concept and adjustment. Major findings have been classified and presented under the following heads:

(i) Findings pertaining to self-concept of students constituted on the basis of sex, residential background, academic stream and level of achievement.

(ii) Findings pertaining to adjustment of students constituted on the basis of sex, residential

background, academic stream and level of achievement.

(iii) Finding pertaining to the inter-relationship between all possible pairs of variables.

1. Findings pertaining to self-concept of students constituted on the basis of sex, residential background, academic streams and level of achievements.

(a) In respect of hypothesis one (H_1), it was found that the global self-concept of the male students was not significantly different from that of the female students. But the sex difference was found to be significant in respect of physical, social, educational, moral and intellectual dimensions of self-concept. It was found that male students had better physical, educational and intellectual self-concepts than the female students. On the other hand female students displayed better social and moral self-concepts than the male students. However, than the male students sex did not emerge as an important determinant of student's temperamental self-concept.

(b) In respect of hypothesis two (H_2), it was found that the difference between the means of the total self-concept scores of the urban and rural students was not significant. This lack of difference existed even when the urban students were compared with rural students in terms of physical, temperamental and moral dimensions of the self-concept. However, on the individual dimensions of the self-concept, namely, social educational and intellectual the urban-rural differences were significant. The urban students in comparison to their rural counterparts had better

educational and intellectual self-concepts while the rural students had better social self-concept than the urban students.

(c) By testing H_3 it was found that the global self-concept of the arts students was not significantly different from that of the science students. This lack of difference existed even when the arts students were compared with science students in terms of their physical, social, temperamental and moral dimensions of self-concept.

However, the difference between the means of the self-concept scores of the arts and science students was significant and the differences were in favour of arts students.

It was further found that the global self-concept of the arts students was significantly different from that of the commerce students and the difference was in favour of arts students. Such difference was also noticed in case of social, temperamental, educational, moral and intellectual dimensions of self-concept. The arts students in comparison to the commerce students had better temperamental, educational, moral and intellectual self-concepts, on the other, hand the commerce students as compared to arts students had better social self-concept. However, the arts and commerce students did not differ significantly on their physical dimension of self-concept.

When the science and commerce students were compared, it was found that there were significant differences on educational and moral dimensions of self-concept and even on global self-concept. These differences were in favour of the science students. On the physical, social, temperamental and intellectual dimension of self-concept these two groups (i.e., science vs. commerce) did not differ significantly.

(d) Regarding H_7, striking differences were observed in the mean scores of high and low achievers with regard to temperamental, educational, moral and intellectual dimensions of self-concept and total self-concept and the differences were in favour of high achievers. However, there were no significant differences between the high and low achievers with respect to their physical and social self-concepts.

2. Findings pertaining to adjustment of students constituted on the basis of sex, residential background, academic stream and level of achievements.

(a) By testing H_4, it was found that the difference between the means of the total adjustment scores of the male and female students was not significant. This lack of difference was also existed between the male and female students in the emotional and educational adjustment areas. However, sex difference was found to be significant in social adjustment. It was found that female students were well-adjusted than the male ones in their social settings/ interactions.

(b) In respect to H_5, it was found that the difference between the means of the total adjustment scores of the urban and rural adolescents was significant and the differences was in favour of urban students indicating better adjustment ability of the urban student. In the areas of educational adjustment, the urban students were found to be superior than their rural counterparts. Both the groups, however occupied the similar position in case of emotional adjustment and social adjustment.

(c) In respect of H_6, it was found that the total adjustment of the science students was significantly different from that of the arts students and the difference favoured the science students. Such difference also existed in all the areas of adjustment, namely emotional, social and educational and the differences were in favour of science students.

When the arts students were compared with the commerce students, it was found that the difference between the means of the total adjustment scores of both the groups were not significant. Such insignificant difference was also noted in case of emotional adjustment. However, the arts and commerce students differed significantly in their social and educational adjustment. The arts students, as compared to the commerce students, had better educational adjustment while the commerce students had better social adjustment than the arts students.

In comparison to the commerce students, the science students had better overall adjustment. The science students were also found to be superior in their emotional and educational adjustment than the commerce students. However, these two groups of students (i.e., science and commerce) were found to be alike in their social adjustment.

(d) By testing H_8, it was found that the total adjustment pattern of the high achievers was significantly different from that of the low achievers and the difference was in favour of the high achievers. Similar was the result in case of the three areas of adjustment (i.e., emotional, social, and educational). As a whole, the high achievers had better adjustment than the low achievers.

3. Findings pertaining to the inter-relationship between all possible pairs of variables.

(a) Regarding H_9, a positive and significant correlation between total self-concept and academic achievement was found. It was also

found that the correlations of academic achievement with the four dimensions of self-concept (i.e., temperamental, educational, moral and intellectual) were positive and significant at 0.01 level of significance. However, the correlation between educational self-concept and academic achievement was found to be stronger.

But there was no correlation between achievement and physical self-concept and between achievement and social self-concept.

(b) By testing H_{10}, it was found that a positive and significant correlation existed between over-all adjustment and academic achievement. It was also found that the correlations of academic achievement with all the areas of adjustment, namely emotional, social and educational were positive and significant. However, the correlation between the educational adjustment and academic achievement was stronger.

(c) Regarding H_{11}, a positive and significant correlation between self-concept and adjustment was found. There was significant relationship between emotional adjustment and four dimensions of self-concept (i.e., temperamental, educational, moral and intellectual). Even the total self-concept was significantly related with emotional adjustment of the students. The relationship between educational self-concept and emotional adjustment was stronger. However, the relationship of physical and social self-concepts with emotional adjustment were not significant.

Similarly, social adjustment was significantly related with all the dimensions of self-concept and total self-concept.

However the relationship between these two variables was found to be moderate. The correlation between social self-concept and social adjustment was stronger.

There was significant but positive correlation between educational adjustment and four dimensions of self-concept, namely, temperamental, educational, moral and intellectual. Even the total self-concept was significantly related to educational adjustment of the students. The relationship of educational self-concept with educational adjustment was found to be stronger, it was further found that the physical self-concept of the students was not significantly related with their total adjustment.

EDUCATIONAL IMPLICATIONS

No research effort can be said to be worthwhile if it does not emanate some of the important educational implications. The implications based on the findings of the study are given below.

1. The present study found sex difference in some dimensions of self-concept. In the Indian cultural matrix there tends to be sex difference in the various dimensions of self-concept. Therefore, the teachers and guidance workers should find out the causes for which the boys and girls differ in various dimensions of self-concept. They should also suggest the remedies for developing physical, educational and intellectual dimensions of self-concept among the female students. Similarly ways and means should be found out to encourage the male students to develop their social and moral self-concepts.

2. Although residential background of the students did not affect their self-concept, yet in some dimensions of self-concept rural-urban difference was significant. It was found that the rural students had lower educational and intellectual self-concepts than the urban students. Therefore, the educational institutions situated in rural areas should draw up a special plan, like guidance programme, to boost

up the educational and intellectual self-concepts so that the academic results are improved. Further, the government should provide more educational amenities to cerate enriched environment in colleges situated in rural areas so that such self-concepts of the students studying there may be developed.

3. The present study found the influence of academic stream on the various dimensions of self-concept. Hence human relation groups, involvement of students in decision-making, relevant curricula, class-room interaction, video techniques etc. should be designed to improve the students self-concept.

4. One of the results of the study indicated that the high achievers were superior in their self-concept in general and temperamental, educational, moral and intellectual, in particular. The following strategies may be evolved for personality development of low achievers.

   - For developing self-concept of low achieving students on their intellectual status, creative work, problem-solving games, essay competitions, debates, quizzes, and group discussions should be introduced on a large scale in colleges.
   - Due recognition and appreciations in the above activities should be given by distribution of awards, prizes, scholarships and medals.
   - Self-concept of these students on educational status can be built up and raised by developing a feeling of belongingness towards their institutions. Association should be formed in various subjects and each student be assigned some responsibility.
   - Organization of varied types of functions, extra-mural talks and curricular programmes provide excellent opportunities for sharing responsibilities and thereby gaining a position

of status. This would raise their self-concept on moral, temperamental and educational status.

- Counselling services should be arranged for these students.
- Sensitivity training programmes should be arranged periodically for solving emotional problems of these students and thereby raising their self-concept on temperamental status, which, in turn, leads to develop their personality.
- Teachers must help students develop positive self-concept through their approval and interpersonal relations.
- Courses in human behavour, interpersonal relations, motives and self-understanding should be introduced at the higher secondary stage.
- Congenial academic atmosphere should be evolved in the colleges.

5. The sample students constituted on the basis of their sex, residential background and academic streams, have shown different types of adjustment problems. The male students had poor social adjustment than the female students. For the purpose different types of co-curricular programmes should be organized. The rural students had more adjustment problems than the urban students. The causes of such adjustment problems should be identified and efforts must be made to help these students to overcome them. The educational institution should feel a strong responsibility for the rural adolescents' welfare. It should make a genuine effort to help all such students in becoming well-adjusted. Similarly students belonging to different academic streams have their unique adjustment

problems. In this context, counseling services can help a lot.

6. The results obtained in this study point to the importance of harmonious pattern of adjustment to the emotional, social and educational situations which underlie academic achievement. The over-achievers as a group significantly differed from the under-achievers with regard to their patterns of adjustment to the emotional, social and educational situations. It is not unnatural or abnormal to have problems. Successfully living consists in meeting the problems of adjustment squarely, students have their shared of problems peculiar to themselves. Some of their problems arise from within themselves and some emanate from the collegiate situation in which the students find themselves. Since academic performance is significantly affected by the nature of adjustment, ways and means have to be found to help students to make desirable adjustment. This has a great practical implication from the point of view the educationist and administrator. Much of the needless educational waste could be avoided by instituting suitable remedial programmes. In this context, paying special attention to secure better adjustment on the part of the students assumes great significance. This is one of the most promising ways of increasing the efficiency of students and securing to society the enduring values of education.

A significantly large number of problems reported by the under-achievers are in the area of motivation. If academic failure is to be forestalled and standards improved, it is inescapable that colleges should provide relevant values and stimulating academic environments. Students often acquire unworthy and inappropriate values through informal association with undesirable influences of their peer groups. Such students, however, could be encouraged to find a member of the faculty with whom they can with facility establish a relaxed intellectual companionship. What is urgently required is the creation of an atmosphere conducive to intellectual excellence and constant vigilance to counter and over-come psychological inertia and growing cynicism in our students during the crucial phase in their development when they stay at the seats of higher learning.

7. The self-concept has been found to affect academic achievement. This trend has already been established through the differential analysis of high and low achievers in terms of their self-concept. The reasons for differences in achievement lie in the way one looks to oneself, thus governing the motivational level which directly affects achievement. Therefore, attempts need to be taken to develop the students' intrinsic motivation.

8. It was further found that the adjustment patterns affects the achievement of the students. Guidance workers and counsellors need to pay special attention to help, guide and improve their conditions so that they may develop into healthy personalities, by eliminating the kinds of problems they face in their home and school etc. and achieve more.

9. This study showed that there was strong relationship between self-concept and adjustment. Good self-concept depends largely on good adjustment and vice-versa. Therefore, it is needless to say that the self-concept and adjustment ability of the students should be taken care of. The different problems encountered by these students should be resolved by the appropriate authority.

So educational institutes should provide guidance services to help students solve their problems related with self-concept and adjustment because the educational institutions to day aim at all-round and harmonious development of students' personality and not merely imparting bookish knowledge.

SUGGESTIONS FOR FURTHER RESEARCH

In the light of present study the following suggestions are offered for further research.

1. This study may be replicated on larger samples and in other states taking students of different stages of education and from different types of institutions so as to examine the phenomenon in further details.

2. A study may be planned and undertaken to predict pupil achievement on the basis of their adjustment, self-concept besides other relevant variables.

3. Case studies may be conducted for acquiring in-depth knowledge into the phenomenon of high and low achievement.

4. Studies may be conducted to ascertain the influence of varying institutional climate and home environment on students' self-concept and adjustment in relation to their level of achievement.

5. Longitudinal studies may be conducted to study the impact of background variables of students on their self-concept and adjustment.

6. Cross-cultural studies of these variables among students in Indian and some foreign countries may be attempted.

7. More objective assessment of self-concept and adjustment can be made by using some other forms of tests and techniques.

8. Similar studies may be conducted by controlling the intervening variables like cast, culture and socio-economics status.

Bibliography

Adler, A. (1931). *Problems of Neuroses,* New York: Cosmopolitan Book Corporation.

Agarwal, R. and Sonawat, R. (1991). "Discipline-wise Comparison of Adjustment of College Students", *Trends in Education,* XXII.

Agarwal, R. (1994). "The Relationship Between Sex and General Self-Concept in Grade IX Student", *Bharatiya Shiksha Shodh Patrika,* 13(2), 17-22.

Akirt, R.V. (1959). "Inter-relationship among Various Dimensions of Self-concept", *Journal of Counselling Psychology,* 6(3), 491-493.

Alexander, A.S. (1955). *Personality Adjustment and Mental Health.* New York: Rine Hart Inc., 429.

Allport, G.W. (1962). *Personality: A Psychological Interpretation.* London: Constable and Co.

Aminabhavi, V.A. (1996). "A Study of Adjustment Ability of Physically Disabled and Able Students," *Journal of Community Guidance and Research.* 13(1), 13-17.

Anderson, J.R. (1954). "Do College Students Lack Motivation? Or are they Motivated to Fail?" *Personality and Guidance Journal,* 33, 209-210.

Aniloff, L. (1977). "The Relationship Between High School Programme and Self-concept, Occupational Aspiration and Occupational Expectation among Nineth Grade Students." *Dissertation Abstract International,* 38(6), 3233-A.

Annamma, A.K. (1984). *Values, Aspiraitons and Adjustment of College Students in Kerala.* Ph.D. Psy, Ker. Univ.

Anshu, (1988). "Level of Aspiration, Achievement Motivation and Adjustment of Adolescents: Effect of Family Climate", *Indian Educational Review,* XXIII (4), 97-104.

Arcangelo, K.T. (1992). "An Examination of the Self-perceptions of Interpersonal Relationships and Self-concepts of Learning Disabled Adults," *Dissertation Abstract International,* 52(9), 3219-A.

Arkoff, A. (1968). *Adjustment and Mental Health.* New York: McGraw-Hill. 6.

Asha C.B. (1978). *An Empirical Study of the Adjustment Pattern of Creative Children in Secondary Schools.* Ph.D. Psy, Ker. Univ.

Ausubel, D.P. (1952). *Educational Psychology: A Cognitive View.* New York: Holt, Rinehart, and Winston.

Babel, M. (1986). *A Study of Adjustment of Foreign Students Studying in the Universities of Rajasthan,* Ph.D. Edu. Moh. Sukh. Univ.

Baldwin, J.M. (1895). *Mental Development in the Child and the Race.* New York: Macmillan.

Banks, O. and Finlayson, D. (1973). *Success and Failure in the Secondary School: An Inter Disciplinary Approach to School Achievement,* London: Methuen and Co. Ltd.

Barry, C.T. (1991). "The Relationship among Domains of Self-concept and Academic Achievement in Learning-disabled Children." *Dissertation Abstract International,* 52(3), 842-A.

Beasley, J. (1957). *Underachievement: Review of the Literature* Talented Youth Project, H.M.L.I., Teachers' College, New York: Columbia University.

Beaty, L.A. (1991). "Psychological Adjustment and Academic Achievement of Visually Handicapped University Students," *Dissertation Abstract International,* 52(6), 2068-A.

Bell, H.M. (1958). *The Adjustment Inventory (Adult form)*—Manual Alto, California Consulting Psychologist Press.

Bell, S.L.M. (1991). "Student Attributions for Social and Academic Success and Failure and their Relationships with Self-concept, Social Functioning and Achievement," *Dissertation Abstract International,* 52(3), 843-A.

Bertocci, P.A. (1945). "The Psychological Self, the Ego and Personality," *Psychological Review,* 52, 91-92.

Best, J.W. (1978). *Research in Education.* New Delhi: Prentice Hall of India Pvt. Ltd.

Bhadauria, S.P.C. (1980). *A Comparative Study of Creativity, Self-Concept and Meaning of Success among Gifted and Other Science Students,* Ph.D. Psy., Agra Univ.

Bharathi, G. (1984). *A Study of Self-concept and Achievement Motivation of Early Adolescents,* Ph.D. Psy., Osm. Univ.

Bhardwaj, S.K. (1997). *A Psycho-social Study of Adjustment among Adolescents.* Ph.D., Home Sc., P.R.S. Univ.

Bhatnagar, R.P. (1966). "Academic Achievement as a Function of one's Self-concept and ego Functions", *Journal of Educational and Psychological Review,* 6 (4), 88-99.

Bhatnagar, R.P. (1970). 'A Study of Self-concept of Bright Achievers and Non-achievers", *Journal of Educational and Psychological Review,* 10(3), 137-143.

Bissa, S., Singh, B.G. and Helode, R.D. (1993). "Self-Concept: A Comparison between Blind and Normal Students". *Perspectives in Psychological Researchs,* 16(1&2), 58-60.

Brim, O.G. Jr. (1954). "College Grades and Self-Estimates of Intelligence," *Journal of Educational Psychology,* 45, 477-484.

Boneau, C.A. (1960). "The Effects of Violation of Assumptions Underlying the '*t*' test", *Psychological Bulletin,* I(XII), 62.

Broderick, R.D. (1992). "The Independent Contributions of Friendship and Social Acceptance to the Development and Adjustment of Pre-adolescents," *Dissertation Abstract International,* 52(9), 3221-A.

Brookover, W.B., Paterson, A. and Thomas, S. (1982). *Self-concept of Ability and School Achievement,* Cooperative Research Project No. 845, Michigan, College of Education, Michigan State University.

Buch. M.B. (Ed.), (1987). *Third Survey of Research in Education* (1978-83). New Delhi: N.C.E.R.T,

Buch, M.B. (Ed.), (1991). *Fourth survey of Research in Education* (1983-88), New Delhi: N.C.E.R.T.

Buch M.B (Ed.), (1997) *Fifth Survey of Research in Education* (1988-92). New Delhi: N.C.E.R.T.

Callis, K.E. (1991). "A Programme to Improve Self-concept for Children Living in a Residential Setting," *Dissertation Abstract International,* 52(4), 1257-A.

Campbell, P.B. (1966). "Self-concept and Academic Achievement in Middle Grade Public Children", *Dissertation Abstract International*, A-27.

Campbell, P.C. (1990). "An Investigation of the self-concept and Locus-of-Control of Specific Learning Disables Students". *Dissertation Abstract International,* 51(4), 1192-A.

Cantril. H. (1958). *The Politics of Despair*, New York: Basic Books.

Caplin, M.D. (1968). "Self-concept, level of aspiration and academic achievement," *Journal of Negro Education*, 27, 126-135.

Carroll, H.A. and Jones, H.M. (1944). "Adjustment Problems of College Students in a Teachers College," *School and Society*, 59, 270-272.

Cattell, R.B. (1945). "Personality Traits Associated with Abilities II with Verbal and Mathematical Abilities," *Journal of Education and Psychology*, 51, 475-486.

Chartrand J.M. (1990). "The Consequences of Multiple Role Participation on the Academic and Fersonal Adjustment of Students", *Dissertation Abstract International*, 50(10), 3183-A.

Chaurasia, O. (1993). "Creativity in Relation to Adjustment and Aggression." *Perspectives in Psychological Researches*, 16(1&2), 64-66.

Chein, I. (1944). "The Awareness of Self and the Structure of the ego". *Psychological Review*, 51, 304-314.

Cheng. H.P. (1989). "The Initial Adjustment of Chinese and Korean Graduate Students to a Large University in the United States", *Dissertation Abstract International*, 49(11) 3267-A.

Chouhan, V and Murthy, S. (1994). "Effect of Achievement on Adjustment of Deprived Adolescents." *Phycho-Lingua*, 24(1), 49-53.

Christensen C.M. (1956). "A note on Borow's Inventory of Academic Adjustment," *Journal of Educational Research,* 30, 55-58.

Coleman, J.C. (1971). *Psychology and Effective Behaviour,* Bombay: D.B. Taraporevala Sons and Co. Pvt. Ltd.

Combs, A.W. and Soper, D.W. (1957). "The Self, its Derivative Terms and Research" *Journal of Individual Psychology,* 13,134-135.

Combs, A.W. and Snygg, D. (1959). *Individual Behaviour: A Perceptual Approach to Behaviour* (Revised Edition) New York: Harper and Brothers, 22.

Congdon, N.A. (1943). "The Perplexities of College Freshmen" *Educational Psychological Measurement*, 3, 367-375.

Cooley, C.H. (1902). *Human Nature and the Social Order*. New York: Scribner.

Coopersmith, S. (1967). *The Antecedent of Self-esteem*. San Francisco: Freeman.

Corson, H.F. (1927). "Factor in the Development of Psychoses in Collegemen," *Mental Hygiene,* 11, 498-518.

Crow, L.D. and Crow, A. (1956). *Understanding Our Behaviour*. New York: Alfred A. Knoff.

Darlington, H. Jr. (1978). "The Effect of Physical Education on the Self-concept of Preserve Elementary Education Majors," *Dissertation Abstract International*, 38(8), 4744.

Davidson, H.H. and Lang. G. (1960). "Children Perception of their Teachers Feelings Toward them Related to Self-Perception, School Achievement and Behaviour". *Jr. Edp. Edu*. 29, 107-118

Deo, P. and Sharma, S. (1970). "Self-concept and School Achievement," *Indian Educational Review,* 5(1), 100-105.

Dinkmeyer, D.C. (1965) *Child Development the Emerging Self*. Univ. Press: De Paul University.

Divine. J.H. (1975). "An Investigation in to the Relationship Between Self-Esteem and Reading Achievement," *Dissertation Abstract International*, 36(3,4). 2095-A.

Dutt. M.L. (1987). "Adjustment—A Conceptual Frame Work". *Experiments in Education*, XV(2), 11-17.

Estridge, P.C. (1989). "The Effects of Academic Placement on Adjustment of Students as Measured by the California Test of Personality", *Dissertation Abstract International,* 49(7), 1701-A.

Ferguson, G.A. and Takane, Y. (1989). *Statistical Analysis in Psychology and Education,* New York: McGraw-Hill Book Co.

Flurkey, J.M. (1978). "The Relationship of Open Education to Students Academic Self-concept and Teacher Style," *Dissertation Abstract International*, 38(8), 4567-A.

Fox, L.S. (1990). "The Effects of Relocation and Family Structure upon Academic Achievement and Behavioural Adjustment of 14 Eighth Grade Students," *Dissertation Abstract International*, 50(9), 2834-A.

Frankel, E. (1960). "A Comparative Study of Achieving and Under Achieving High School Boys of Higher Intellectual Ability," *Journal of Educational Research,* 50, 172-180.

Frederick, J.M. (1975). *Educational Psychology,* New York: Overseas Publication Ltd., 469

French, J.W. (1958). "Validation of New Item Types Against four Years Academic Criteria," *Journal of Educational Psychology,* 49, 67-76.

Freud, S. (1935). *A General Introduction to Psychoanalysis,* New York: Liveright.

Gallenghar, J.T. (1964). *Teaching the Gifted Child.* Boston: Allyn and Bacon.

Garrett, H.E. (1949). "A Review and Interpretation of Investigation's of Factors Related to Scholastic Success in Colleges of Art and Sciences at Teachers College", *Jr. Exp. Educ.* 28, 91-138.

Garrett. H.E. (1971). *Statistics in Psychology and Education.* Bombay: Vakils, Feffer, and Simons Pvt. Ltd.

George, E.I. (1966). *A comparative study of the adjustment and achievement of 10 years and 11 years Schooling in Kerla State,* Dept. of Psy., Kerla. U. (UGC Financed).

Good, C.V. (Ed.), (1959). *Dictionary of Education.* New York: Macmillan.

Goswami, N. (1980). *Adjustment problems of school going Adolescent Girls and the Development of an Adjustment Inventory for their measurement,* Ph.D. Edu., Gau. Univ.

Goswami, P.K. (1980). "A Study of Self-concept of Adolescents and its Relationship to Scholastic Achievement", *Indian Educational Review.* XI(1), 95-98.

Grogon, R.B. (1977). "A Comparative Study of the Openness of the Learning Environment, Student Achievement and Student self-concept as Learner in an Open Space School and Non-Open Space School", *Dissertation Abstract International,* 37(7), 4115-A.

Grzegorek, H.L.M. (1990). "A study of Self-Concept and Obesity in Adult Females", *Dissertation Abstract International,* 52(5), 1690-A.

Guidry, P.L. (1990). "Adolescents with Cystic Fibrosis: Effects of Cognitive Problem Solving Skills and Interpersonal Relationships on Adjustment", *Dissertation Abstract International*, 50(8), 2430-A.

Guilford. J.P. and Fruchter, B. (1985). *Fundamental Statistics in Psychology and Education*, Singapore: McGraw-Hill International Book Co.

Gupta, A.K. (1981). *A Study of Parental Preference in Relation to Adolescent's Personality Adjustment and Achievement*, Model Institute of Education and Research, Jammu (NCERT Financed).

Gupta, P. (1984) *Self-concept, Dependency and Adjustment Pattern of Abandoned Institutionalized Preadolescents*, PhD., Appl., Psy., Cal. Univ.

Harper, K.L. (1990). "An Investigation of Inferred and Professed Self-concept As-learner of Gifted and Average Middle School Students," *Dissertation Abstract International*, 51(3), 727-A.

Hatfield, A.B. (1961). "An Experimental Study of the Self-concept of Student Teachers," *Junior Education Research*, 55(2), 87.

Haynes, R.A. (1990). Relationships between Adjustment and Attitudes Towards Cooperation, Competition, and Individualism in Individuals between the Ages of Twenty-one and Sixty-five," *Dissertation Abstract International*, 51(5), 1552-A.

Hibler, F.W. and Larson, A.H. (1944), "Problems of Upper Class Students in a Teachers College," *Journal of Applied Psychology*, 59, 270-272.

Hilgard, E.R. (1949), "Human Motives and the Concept of the Self," *American Psychologist*, 9, 374-382.

Hillway, T. (1956). *Introduction to Research*. Boston: Houghton Mifflin.

Holland, J.L. and, Astin, A.W.(1962). "The Prediction of the Academic, Artistic, Scientific and Social Achievement of Under-Graduates of Superior Scholastic Aptitude, *Journal of Education and Psychology*, 53, 132-148.

Horrall, B.M. (1957). "Academic Performance and Personality Adjustment of Highly Intelligent College Students", *Genel. Psy., Monogr.*, 55, 3.

Houston, W.M. and Marzolf, S.S. (1944), "Faculty use of the Problem Check List", *Journal of Higher Education* 15, 325-328.

Hurlock, E. (1955). *Adolescent Development*. New York: Mc-Graw Hills Co.

James, B. and Lobeck, R. (1961). "Self-concept Differences in Relation to Identification, Relation and Social Class", *Journal of Abnormal and Social Psychology*, 62(1), 94-96.

James, W. (1980). *The Principles of Psychology*, New York: Holt, Rinehart, and Winston Inc.

James, P.F. (1991). "Perceived Support, Self-concept and Academic Achievement of Black Sub-urban High School Students", Dissertation *Abstract International*, 52(8), 2864-A.

Jayaswal, V.K. (1973). A Study of Self-concept in Relation to Age-Sex Differences, M.Ed. Dissertation, H.P. University.

Jersild, A.T. (1952). *In Search of Self*, New York: Bureau of Publication, Teachers College, Columbia University, 114.

Jersild, A.T. (1954). *Child Psychology*, Englewood Cliffs: N.J.: Prentice Hall, 179.

Jogawar, V.V. (1976). *Development of Self-concept in Relation to some Family Factors at the Adolescence Level*, Ph.D. Edn., Nagpur University.

Johnson, W.H. (1978). "A Comparative Study of the Achievement, Motivation and Self-concept of High School Students in Open-Space and Self-contained Class-Room,"· *Dissertation Abstract International*, 38(9), 5220-A.

Joshi, M.C. and Pandey, J. (1964). *Adjustment Inventory*, (Mimeographed Information), New Delhi: NCERT.

Kaile, H.S. and Kaur, R. (1995). "Adjustment of over and under achievers in mother tongue," *Experiments in Education*, XXIII (2), 33-38.

Kamalesh, A. (1981). *A Comparative study of Self-concept. Adjustment Interests and Motivation among the Scheduled Caste and Non-Scheduled Caste Students*, Ph.D. Edu. Kan. Univ.

Kapoor, R. (1987). Study of Factors Responsible for High and Low Achievement at the Junior High School Level, Ph.D. Edu., Avadh Univ.

Kasinath, H.M. (2000). "A Study of Students Adjustment and its Relation to Organizational Climate in Jawahar Navodaya Vidyalayas," *Quest in Education*, XXIV(3), 30-38.

Keith, E.C. (1970). "Difference Between self-concept of Disadvantaged and Non-Disadvantaged High School Students with in Certain type of Rural and Urban Communities," *Dissertation Abstract International*, 31, 1015-A.

Kelley, A. (1978). "Self-concept and Career Selection of Black Community College Students," *Dissertation Abstract International*, 38(6), 2941-A.

Keshap, B.R. (1993). *A Study of Motivational Pattern Adjustment and Attitude Towards Study of College Students*. Ph.D. Edu., Saurashtra Univ.

Kipins, D.N. (1961), "Change in Self-concept in Relation to Perception of Others," *Journal of Personality*, 29, 449-465.

Kubiniec, C.M. (1970). "The Relative Efficiency of Various Dimensions of the Self-concept in Predicting Academic Achievement, *American Educational Research Journal*, 7, 321-336.

Kukreti, B.N. (1994). "Adjustment of Preadolescent students of Saraswati Vidya Mandir, Convent School and Government Junior High School: A Comparative Study". *Bharatiya Shiksha Shodh Partrika,* 13(2), 5-14.

Kumar, D., Prasad, S.K. and Prasad, B. (1995). "A Study of Adjustment Pattern of Physically Handicaps" *Perspectives in Psychological Researches*, 17 and 18(1&2) 53-55.

Kumar, D., Singh, V. and Mohamad, T. (1995). "Effect of Community, Caste and Faculty on Adjustment/Maladjustment of Adolescents, *Perspectives in Psychological Researches*, 17 and 18(1&2), 39-41.

Kumar, S. (1985). *A Comparative Study of the Interests, Needs, and Adjustment Problems of Gifted and Average Children*, Ph.D. Edu., Del. Univ.

Kumari, S. (1982). *A Study of Intelligence, Achievement, Adjustment and Socio-economic Patterns of Different Socio-metric Groups of Adolescents* Ph.D. Edu., Pan. Univ.

Kurtz, J.J. and Swenson, E. (1951) Factors Related to Over Achievement and Under-Achievement in School," *School Review,* 59, 472-480.

Lall, A.S. (1978). "A Comparison of Job Corps Graduates and Non-Job Corps Graduates with Respect to Selected Academic and Psychological Variables", *Dissertation Abstract International*. 37(11), 7014-A.

Lata, K. (1985). *Impact of Parental Attitude on Social, Emotional and Educational Adjustment of Normal and Handicapped Students*, Ph.D. Psy., Agra. Univ.

Lazarus, R.S. (1976). *Patterns of Adjustment.* Tokyo: McGraw-Hill (3rd ed.), 15.

Lecky, P. (1945). *Self-Consistency: A Theory of Personality*, New York: Island Press.

Lehner, G.F.J. and Kube, E. (1964). *The Dynamic of Adjustment*, N.J., Prentice Hall.

Lindquist, E.F. (1968). *Statistical Analysis in Educational Research*, New Delhi: Oxford and IBH Publishing Co.

Lindzey, G. and Hall, C.S. (1957). *Theories of Personality*, New York: John Wiley.

Lou, H. (1990). "A Study of Adjustment Problems of Chinese Students in Selected Higher Education Institutions in U.S.," *Dissertation Abstract International*, 50(10, 3165-A.

Lundholm, H. (1940). "Reflections upon the Nature of the Psychological Self," *Psychological Review*, 47, 110-127.

Lynche, M.D., Norem, H.A.A. and Gergen, K.J. (1981). *Self-Contemplations-Self-Concept: Advance in Theory and Research*, Cambridge: Mass Ballinger.

Maikhuri, R. and Pande, S.K. (1997). "Self-Concept of adolescents in Relation to their Academic Achievement," *Psycho-Lingua*, 27 (2), 121-124.

Malarczyk, B.B. (1990). "Academic Achievement and Self-Concept of Military Adolescents Attending Canadian Department of National Defense Schools," *Dissertation Abstract International*, 50(12), 3899-A.

Manju, T. (1994). *Adjustment as a Function of Sense of Humour, Degree of Aggression and Inferiority Feelings*, Ph.D. Psy., Meerut University.

Martel, J.H. (1990). "Black Student Self-concept and Academic Performance: An Analysis of an Urban middle School District." *Dissertation Abstract International*, 51(6), 1979-A.

Martin, M. (1991). "The Self-Concept and Locus-of-Control of Learning Disables College Students," *Dissertation Abstract International*, 52(4), 1267-A.

Mary, C. (1989). "A Participant Observation Study to Describe and Explain what Occurs in a Behaviour and Adjustment Class," *Dissertation Abstract International*, 49(9), 2621-A.

Maslow, A.H. (1968). *Toward a Psychology of Being*, New York: Van Nostrand.

Mattoo, B.K. (1980), "Social and Emotional Adjustment Patterns of Adolescent Boys and Girls at Various Levels of Socio-Economic Status and General Intelligence", *Indian Educational Review*, XV(I), 110-114.

McCandless, B.R. (1961). *Children and Adolescents*, New York: Holt, Rinehart and Winston, 190.

McGough, R.L. (1978). "The Relationship of Self-concept, Meaning and Value of Work of Disadvantages and Non-Disadvantaged Eleventh Grade Students". *Dissertation Abstract International*, 38(8), 4773-A.

Mckay, S.E. (1990), "Psycho-social Competence, Adjustment to College, and Academic Success of Learning-disabled Community College Students," Dissertation Abstract International, 51(4), 1167-A.

McKinney, F. (1941). *Psychology of Personal Adjustment*, New York: John Wiley and Sons Inc.

Mead, G.H. (1903). "The Social Self", *Journal of Philosophy* 5(2), 374-380.

Mehta, P.H. (1968). "The Self-concept of Bright Underachieving Male High School Students" *Indian Educational Review*, 3(2), 81-86.

Miller, G.A. (1962). *Psychology: The Science of Mental Life*, New York: Harper and Row.

Minnalkodi, B. (1997) "*A Study of Higher Secondary School Students, Achievement in Zoology in Relation to Anxiety, Achievement-Motivation and Self-concept*", Ph.D. Education, Annamalai University.

Mittelmeier, C.M. (1989). "Correlates of Adjustment among Children Referred for a Learning Disability Evaluation", *Dissertation Abstract International*, 49(5), 1256-A.

Morgan, H.H. (1952). 'A psychometric Comparison of Achieving and Non-achieving College Students of High Ability" *Journal of Consult. Psychology*, 16, 292-298.

Moulton, K.C. (1990). "An Analysis of the Impact of a Social Skills Intervention on the Self-concept Academic Achievement and Behavioural Patterns of Seventh Grade at-risk Students", *Dissertation Abstract International*, 51(4), 1168-A.

Mouly, G.J. (1964). *The Science of Educational Research*, New Delhi: Eurasia Publishing House Pvt. Ltd.

Mouly, G.J. (1973). *Psychology for Effective Teaching*, New York: Holt Rinehart and Winston Inc., 85-86.

Murphy, G. (1947). *Personality A Bio-Social Approach to Origins and Structure*, New York: Harper and Row.

Nair, P.V. (1999). "Certain Personality and Familial Variables Discriminating between over and Underachievers in Secondary Schools Science and Mathematics", *Experiment in Education*, XXVII(II), 14-23.

Nosan, L.J. (1958). *Academic Achievement of Gifted High School Students*, Los Angels: Calif. University of Southern California Press.

Nayal, S. et.al (1989). "Self-concept and Class Adjustment of Adolescents in Relation to their Sex, School, Discipline, Income Group and Academic Achievement," *Indian Educational Review*, XXIV(2), 105-114.

Nomani, H.R. (1965). *Social-psychological Study of Adjustment of the Adivasi Students*, The Bihar Tribal Welfare Research Institute.

Paderson, D.M. (1965). "Ego Strength and Discrepancy between Conscious and Unconscious Self-concept", *Perceptual and Motor Skills*, 20, 691-692.

Pandey, A., (1970). *A Study of Adjustment Personality, Values and Vocational Interests of Supernormal and Normal Adolescents*, Ph.D. Psy., Agra University.

Pandey, B.B. (1979). *A Study of Adjustment Problem of Adolescent Boys of Deoria and Their Educational Implications*, Ph.D. Edu., Gor. University.

Pandit, I. (1985). *A Study of the Psychological Needs and Self-Concept of Adolescents and their Bearing on Adjustment*, Ph.D. Edu., Bombay University.

Panwar, P.S. (1986). *Roles of Academic Achievement and School Background in Self-concept, Self-disclosure and Inferiority Feeling among Students of Kumaun Hills*. Ph.D. Education Kum. University.

Parween, S. (1955). "A Study of Adjustment among Disadvantaged Students". *Perspective in Psychological Researches*, 17 and 18 (1&2), 56-58.

Payne, D.A. (1962). "Concurrent and Predictive Validity of an Objectives Measurement of Academic Self-Concept" *Educational Psychology Measurement,* 22, 773-780.

Piaget, J. (1932). *The Moral Judgement of the Child*, London: Kegan Paul.

Raimy, V. (1948), "Self Reference in Counselling Interview", *Journal of Consult Psychology*, 4(2) 153-165, 315-317.

Rajamankkam, M. and Vasanthal, R. (1993) "Adjustment Problems of Adolescent Students in Relation to their Achievements". *Journal of Community Guidance and Research*, 10(2), 153-183.

Ramkumar, V. (1970). "Intelligence and Self-concept", *Education and Psychology Review*, 10(3), 154-157.

Ramkumar, V. (1972). "An Investigation into the Relationship of Size of Family to Self-concept and Academic Achievement", *Education and Psychology Review*, 12(3&4), 107-113.

Ramkumar, V. (1979). *Subject Characteristics of Adolescent Girls with Actual Self-concept*, Dept. of Edu., Ker. Univ.

Rangappa, K.T. (1994). "Effect of Self-concept on Achievement in Mathematics" *Psycho-Lingua*, 24(1), 43-48.

Rao, S.N. (1965). "Problems of Adjustment and Academic Achievement", *Journal of Vocational and Educational Guidance*, 10, 40-68.

Rao, S.N. (1967). *Student's Performance and Adjustment*, Tirupati, S.V. University.

Rawat, L. (1995). *A Study of the Effect of Parent Absence on Adjustment, Study Habits and Academic Development of Students of High School Classes*". Ph.D. Edu., Hemwati Nandan Bahuguna Garhwal University.

Razavi, R.A. (1989). "A Study of the adjustment problems of international students in Northern Virginia Community

College, Prince George's Community College and Montgomery College, *Dissertation Abstract International*, 50(5), 1256-A.

Reddy, M.A.B. and Sudha, B.G. (1980), "Adjustment of SC and Non SC Students". *The Indian Journal of Social Work,* XLI(I), 51-57.

Reeder, T. (1955). *A Study of Some Relationship between Level of Self-concept, Academic Achievement and classroom Adjustment*". Unpublished Doctoral Dissertation, North Texas State College.

Richards, J.M. Jr., Cline, V.B. and Abe. C. (1963). "Use of a Biographical Information Blank in the Prediction of Achievement in High School Science", *Educational Psychology Measurement*, 23, 789-798.

Rogers, C.R. (1951). *Client Centered Therapy—Its Current Practices, Implications and Theory,* Boston: Houghton Mifflin.

Rongali, S.P. (1993). *A Study of Adjustment in Relation to Social Integration and Achievement of the Students of Residential Schools*, Ph.D Edn. Andhra University.

Rowand, B.B. (1989). "Perceptions of Academic Ability and Self-concept Among Gifted Achieving and Underachieving Adolescents". Ed.D. University of Georgia.

Sarabin, T. (1953), Role Theory, In G. Lindzey (Ed.), *Hand Book of Social Psychology 1*, Reading Mass Addison Weslay.

Saraswat, R.K. and Gaur, J.S. (1981). "Approaches for the Measurement of Self-Concept—An Introduction," *Indian Educational Review*, 16(3), 114-119.

Sarasota, R.K. (1986). "Adjustment of Adolescents". *Indian Educational Review*, 29(4), 106-111.

Saraswat, R. (1987). *A Student of Self-concept in Relation to Adjustment Values, Academic Achievement, Socio-Economic Status and Sex of High School Students of Delhi*, Ph.D., Soc. II, T. New Delhi.

Saun, G.S. (1980). *Patterns of Self-disclosure and Adjustment among High and Low Achievers* Ph.D. Psy., Kum. Univ.

Saxena, S.K. (1981). *Self-concept, Study Habit and School Attitude as Correlates of Socio-economic Status and Cultural Setting in different Divisionary and Failure of High School Students of Kanpur District,* Ph.D. Edu., Agra., Univ.

Schineiders, A.A. (1955). *Personal Adjustment and Mental Health*, New York: Holt, Rinehart and Winston.

Seaward, M.R. (1977). "A comparison of the Career Maturity, Self-Concept and Academic Achievement of Female Cooperative Vocational Office Training Students, Intensive Business Training Students and Regular Business Students in Selected High Schools in Mississippi", *Dissertation Abstract International*, 37(7), 4321-A.

Sethy, B.P. (1993). A Study of Adjustment Differences among Adolescent Boys and Girls at different Levels of Academic Achievement. M.Ed. Dissertation, Berhampur University.

Shaffer, L.F. (1936). *The Psychology of Adjustment*. Boston: Houghton Mifflin.

Shaffer, M.D.E. (1990). *The Self-concept of Mainstreamed Hearing-Impaired Students*, Ed.D. University of Northern Colorado.

Shah, J.H (1978). *Relationship of Self-concept to Academic Achievement of Secondary School Pupils*, Dept. of Edu., Sau. U. (Sau. U. Financed).

Sharma, G.R. (1986). "Adjustment Problems of Professional and Non-Professional College Students. A Comparative Study". *Indian Educational Review*, 21(1), 25-34.

Sharma, M. and Mehta, M. (1993). "The Effects of Discordance between Interest and Chosen Curriculum upon Psychological Adjustment and Academic Achievement", *Indian Journal of Psychometric and Education,* 24(1), 25-30.

Sharma, M.C. (1979). *A Psychological Study of Adjustment Problems of Harijans S.C. and Backward Class Students of Agra District*, Ph.D. Psy., Agra Univ.

Sharma, N. and Gakhar, S.C. (1999). "Adjustment of Students of Denominational Schools-A Comparative Study", *The Educational Review*. 105(8), 16-18.

Sharma, R. (1985). *Sub-Culture of College Students as a Function of their Adjustment, Values, Academic Motivation and Attitudes,* Ph.D. Edu., Mee. Univ.

Sharma, R.R. (1983). "Self-Concept and Adjustment as Factors in Academic Achievement", *Indian Educational Review*. 18(2), 46-59.

Shavelson, R.J. et al. (1976). "Self-Concept: Validation of Construct Interpretation", *Review of Educational Research*, 46(3), 407-441.

Shaw, M.C. Edson, K and Bell, H.M. (1962). "The Self-Concept of Bright Under-Achieving High School Students as Revealed by an Adjective Checklist", *Personnel Guide Journal*, 53, 203-208.

Sherif, M. and Cantrill, H. (1947). *The Psychology of Ego-Involvements*, New York: John Wiley and Sons Inc.

Sherif, M. and Sherif, C.W. (1956). *An Outline of Social Psychology*. New York: Harper and Row.

Silverman, R.G. (1978). "An Investigation of Self-Concept in Urban, Sub-Urban and Rural Students with Learning Disabilities". *Dissertation Abstract International*, 38(9), 5398-A.

Singh, B.P. and Singh, G. (1987). "Adjustment Behaviour of Adolescents in Relation to Caste and Surroundings". *Experiments in Education*, XV(9), 176-180.

Singh, R.R. (1981). *Adjustment Problems of the S.C. and S.T. Students in Residential Schools of Rajasthan*, Vidya Bhawan, G.S. Teacher's College, Udaipur, (NCERT Financed).

Sinha, A.K.P. and Singh R.P. (1993). *Manual of Adjustment Inventory*. Agra: National Psychological Corporation.

Sinha, B.P. and Singh, A.K. (1995). "Adjustment as the Factor of Parent's Aggression and Strictness", *Perspectives in Psychological Researches*, 17 and 18(1&3), 93-98.

Sinha, D. (1966). "Some Factors Associated with Success and Failure in University", *Indian Educational Review*, 1, 39-40.

Smith, W.D. and Lebo, D. (1956). "Some Changing Aspects of the Self-concept of Adolescent Males", *Journal of Genetic Psychology*, 88.

Srivastava, A.B.L., and Bhatkulikar, S.C. (1980). Sampling Techniques for Educational Surveys, Paper presented in Training Course in Sample Survey Methods in Education, R.C.E., Bhopal.

Srivastava, N. (1980). *Intelligence, Interest, Adjustment and Family Status as Predictors of Educational Attainment of High School Students*, Ph.D. Education, Gor. Univ.

Stainley, C.S. (1967). *The Antecedents of Self-Esteem*, Freeman; San Francisco.

Steinzor. B (1944). "Rorschach Responses of Achieving and Non-Achieving Students of High Ability". *American Journal of Orthopsychiat,* 14, 494-504.

Stormwold, S.A. and Wrenn, G.G. (1948). "Counselling Students Towards School Adjustment", *Educational and Psychological Measurement*, 8, 57-63.

Sultana, Q.A. (1983). *A Study of Some Factors in Adjustment Patterns of Adolescent Boys and Girls in Bangladesh*, Ph.D. Psy., M.S.U.

Sundararajan, S., Govindarajan, M. and Rajasekar, S. (1994). "Self-Concept and Adjustment Problems of B.Ed. Teacher-trainees", *Experiments in Education*, XXII(2), 27-34.

Sunita, (1986). *Motor Ability as a Factor in Home: Social and Emotional Adjustment in Adolescents*, (13+ to 16+) Ph.D. Psy., Edu., Kur. Univ.

Swain, S.K. and Panda, S.K. (1982). "Adjustment Differences among Adolescents Boys and Girls at different Levels of Academic Achievement", *Journal of Educational Research and Extension*. 19(1), 21-29.

Symonds, P.M. (1964). *The Dynamics of Human Adjustment*, New York: Appleton Century.

Terman, L. and Oden, I. (1947). *The Gifted Child Grows up*, California Stanford University Press.

Thompson, G.M. (1948). "College grades and group Rorschach", *Journal of Applied Psychology*, 32, 398-407.

Trafton, B.F. (1978). "Relationship Between Self-Concept. Learning Attitude, Teacher Rating and Academic Achievement in Grades one Through Eight", *Dissertation Abstract International*, 38(10), 6030-A.

Tripathi, S.L. (1981). *Adjustment Problems of Undergraduates of Varanasi Division*. Ph.D. Edu. Gor. Univ.

Valdivieso, R. (1991). "The Effects of School Racial Composition, Minority Curriculum Offerings, and Academic Programme Enrollment on the self-concept, Locus-of-control, Grades, and Aspirations of Puerto Rican High School Seniors", *Dissertation Abstract International*, 52(3) 876-A.

Verma, M. (1966). *An Introduction to Educational and Psychological Research*. Bombay: Asia Publishing House, 51.

Vasantha, R. (1972). "An Investigation into the Relationship of Size of Family to Self-concept and Academic Achievement" *Education and Psychology Review*", XII(3-4), 107-113.

Vasantha, R. (1974). "Self-concept and Achievement in School Subjects of Prospective University Entrants". In M.B. Buch (Ed.), *A Survey of Research in Education*, 341-342.

Verma, L.K. (1971). "A Study of Self-concept in Relation to Internal External Control and Socio-economic Status of High School Students", *Quest in Education*, 16(2), 139-143.

Vishnoi, K. (1974). "A Study of Personality Adjustment to High and Low Achievers", *Journal of Education and Psychology*, 31(4), 212-216.

Vonhaller, G.B. (1970). *Psychology*, New York: Hougton International. 426.

William, R.L. and Cole, S. (1968). "Self-concept and School Adjustment", *Personal Guidance Journal*, 46.

Wylie, R.C. (1961). *The self-concept*, Lincoln University: Nebraska Press.

Zarghouni, A. (1989). "An Analysis of International Students Adjustment and Academic Success in a Predominantly Black and Predominantly white Urban University". *Dissertation Abstract International*, 49(8), 2118.

Index